Also by Charles Lynch

China, One-Fourth of the World
You Can't Print THAT! Memoirs of a Political Voyeur
Our Retiring Prime Minister
Race for the Rose (Election, 1984)

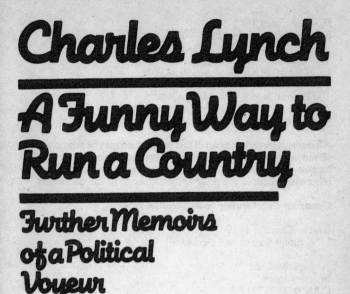

Charles Lynch

A Funny Way to Run a Country

Further Memoirs of a Political Voyeur

A TOTEM BOOK
TORONTO

First published 1986
by Hurtig Publishers Ltd.

This edition published 1987
by TOTEM BOOKS
a division of Collins Publishers
100 Lesmill Road, Don Mills, Ontario

Canadian Cataloguing in Publication Data

Lynch, Charles, 1919-
   A funny way to run a country

1st paperback ed.
Includes index.
ISBN 0-00-217911-3

1. Lynch, Charles, 1919-   - Anecdotes.
2. Canada - Politics and government - Anecdotes, facetiae, satire, etc. 3. Journalists - Canada - Anecdotes, facetiae, satire, etc.
I. Title.

PN4913.L95A3   1987   070'.92'4   C87-094920-9

Designed by David Shaw
Printed and bound in Canada

Contents

*For Claudy, and to the memory of Tommy Douglas,
none of whose jokes is here,
but a lot of his spirit*

A Few Warm-up Pitches

There have been some monumental battles between the CBC and the Canadian Press over how much the people's network should pay each year for the service of the national news service. Out of one memorable set-to, with Dan MacArthur acting for CBC and Gillis Purcell for CP, MacArthur penned some lines that have become a classic description of how a friendly negotiation can turn to ratshit:

> King Huazuaris arose betimes and went down to the mouth of the cave,
> And there he found the Prophet Daniel
> Sitting and reading the Canadian Press report,
> Not that it was then published
> But in order that the scriptures might be fulfilled.
> "How are thou, on the whole?" inquired the king.
> "What hole?" asked the prophet.
> "Asshole," said the king.
> "Kiss it," quoth the prophet.
> "After you," replied the king, with true Oriental courtesy.
> Whereupon they proceeded to throw camel dung at one another, as was the custom in those times.

A former Liberal cabinet minister and his wife were being shown through an apartment they were thinking of buying, and the young lady who was subletting the place obviously wanted to hustle them along. But they wanted to see the whole place, including the master bathroom. The former minister swung the door open and slid back the shower curtain, disclosing the figure of a well-known Conservative Party strategist and adviser.

"Good God," said the former minister, calling the Tory by name. "What are YOU doing here?"

And back came the reply: "I'm voting!"

Pat Carney is the only federal cabinet minister ever to embrace me, and she did it six times in succession. Of course, she wasn't a cabinet minister then — she was running a consultant firm in Yellowknife, and we were flying around the Northwest Territories on a junket.

On our first takeoff from Yellowknife, in the hull of a Hercules transport, Carney was belted into the seat beside me. When they revved up the engines, she threw her arms around me and asked me to hold her tight. Assuming that she was crazed with lust, I gripped her with as much passion as I could muster and we remained locked in hot embrace until airborne, whereupon she loosed her grip and I loosed mine. "Sorry about that," she said, "it's nothing personal. It's just that I hate flying and always have to have something to hang onto at takeoff."

When it came time to let down for the landing, she did it again, and we arrived on the ground in one another's arms, two hearts beating as one. "It's the same thing landing," Carney explained, untangling herself.

On the next takeoff and landing, the performance was repeated, only this time I tried to keep it clinical. But then we switched to a little Cessna bushplane, where the quarters were much closer, and she really cuddled up, though her grip was like a vice. Both of us survived, and she thanked me profusely. We have never flown together since, so I don't know whether she got over her phobia or not. If not, she must be the huggiest cabinet minister ever, anywhere.

One of my favourite stories about Canada's impact in the world involves a tough speech on disarmament made by our chief negotiator, General E. L. M. Burns, the hero of Suez and our first "soldier for peace." Burns's speech was tough on the

Soviets, accusing them of lying about disarmament while arming themselves to the teeth.

Max Ferguson, the resident humorist of CBC Morning at the time under the Rawhide label, invited his listeners to imagine Nikita Khrushchev being roused from his sleep in the Kremlin.

"Vot's new?" inquires a sleepy Khrushchev.

"Tough speech by Canada at Geneva," says an aide.

"Vot they say?"

"They tell us to put up or shut up on disarmament."

"Decisions, decisions! Hokay. Ve put up! Wancouver! Winnipeg! Toronto! Montreal! Five, four, three, two, one! Put up!"

When I told Ferguson, on a platform in Halifax last year, how vividly I remembered that broadcast, he had no recollection of it at all. Nor did he remember a memorable memo from *Maclean's*, after he submitted a requested piece on why he loved Nova Scotia enough to move there from Toronto. It came back with this note: "We asked you to tell us why you love Nova Scotia — not why you hate Toronto!"

Mike Pearson, approaching the last New Year of his life, having lost one eye to cancer, was asked by CBC interviewer Ron Collister if he had a wish for the coming year. "Yes," came the ready reply, with that grin, "I hope I don't lose the other eye."

In that final year I cajoled Pearson into what was promised as a half-hour interview for Ottawa TV station CJOH, and he agreed, though grumbling that in the States, Lyndon Johnson got paid $350,000 for his remembrances. "This is the last one I do for free," said Pearson. We spun the half-hour out into two hours, and broke it into four programs that contained the best of Pearson, though he complained that we conned him.

Within months, he was dead, and when they looked for those tapes at CJOH for the memorial broadcasts, it was discovered that they had been reused to record commercials. Wasn't that supposed to be the beauty of tape over film, that it could be used over and over again?

Pearson is the one prime minister who ever took my advice on anything. For the whole of my lifetime, and long before, there had been agitation in my home town of Saint John, New Brunswick, for a bridge across the harbour. At a political meeting in the 1963 campaign, in full view of the harbour, he turned to me and asked: "Where do you want that bridge?" "Right there," said I, pointing to the spot. "You've got it," said Pearson, and the bridge went up.

John Diefenbaker was a torment to his successor, Robert Stanfield, and he was equally unhappy with the man who replaced Stanfield, Joe Clark. Clark had been in office for more than a month, without consulting Diefenbaker on anything, when suddenly the Old Chief astonished his aides by shouting that he had had enough and wasn't going to stand it any more. "Call a press conference," he commanded, "no more Mr. Nice Guy!" He was dissuaded, but, when he wasn't poring over the arrangements for his own funeral, he kept harping on Clark's shortcomings all through the weeks prior to his death.

Clark paid eloquent tribute at Diefenbaker's grave, but at no point did he call Dief Mr. Nice Guy.

One of Diefenbaker's stories was about Prime Minister Mackenzie King visiting with his minister Chubby Power in Quebec City. Power took King to a cemetery to view the grave of one of King's relatives, and, after a few moments silence, King was heard to mutter: "A fine man, but I hear he voted Tory all his life."

"Don't worry, Prime Minister," chuckled Chubby, "he's voted Liberal in every election since."

Once, when I was chief of Southam News, I was summoned to Halifax by the editor of the Halifax *Chronicle-Herald*, a man named Doc Savage, who wanted to discuss the possibility of his paper taking the Southam service. I appeared at his office at the appointed afternoon hour, only to be informed by him that I had been seen having lunch at the Halifax Press Club, where *Herald* people were forbidden to go. Hence, he said, there was little for us to talk about, especially as I had been heard months before, at Acadia University, saying I would not class the *Herald* as one of Canada's great papers. And he had heard that I appeared occasionally on the CBC, which *Herald* people were forbidden to do, and the head of Southam, St. Clair Balfour, was also president of the Canadian Press, an outfit the *Herald* hated. The *Herald*, need I say, didn't take the Southam service, and hasn't to this day, deeming it too hot to handle.

Long ago, in the provincial liquor store in Chester, Nova Scotia, I advised some visiting Ontario friends not to reveal their home address, so they wouldn't be charged for an out-of-province liquor licence.

When I followed them to the wicket, the clerk's eyes lit up and he called his fellow workers in from the back to greet the "celebrity." After our exchange of compliments and the ritual signing of autographs, the clerk said: "You come on TV from Ottawa, ey? So that will be two dollars for the licence." My friends collapsed, laughing.

Torchy Anderson of Southam News attended a meeting of the Junior Chamber of Commerce and returned to the office with the observation "there's no shirt too young to stuff."

That quotation was attributed to Larry Zolf, whose own best quote doesn't make the record books. That was when Pierre Trudeau announced yet another ad hoc policy, and Zolf exclaimed: "It's ad hockery night in Canada!"

Norman DePoe said news people who wanted to be politicians were like horse players who wanted to be horses, and the quote got claimed by all the talking heads in business, the media, and politics.

Olof Palme, the late prime minister of Sweden, responded to my suggestion that all Canadians are born two drinks below par by saying that all Swedish men are born two drinks short, and all Swedish women are born two drinks above par, while "as for the Finns, none of them has ever been found in a sufficient state of sobriety to establish any basis for comparison."

Former Prime Minister Keith Holyoake of New Zealand advised how to keep his country's lamb from tasting like an old boot: "You thaw it."

Tory Elmer MacKay offered his Central Nova riding to Brian Mulroney because "the Grits in Pictou County are all swank and no knickers."

Yukon bard Robert W. Service, turning up in Vancouver during the war, told me he spent the years between the wars playing the concertina in French whorehouses, "the only places I could find where the residents were bedrock honest."

After years of covering U.N. Secretary General Dag Hammarskjöld and John Diefenbaker, both masters of seeming to say something without saying it, I coined the word "insinuendo." Nobody picked it up.

Nothing being sacred, I parodied our national poem: "To you from failing hands we throw the sponge; be yours to wring it dry."

Maestro Lazslo Gati, then of the Windsor Symphony across from Detroit, found me, as his guest harmonica soloist, unequal to the challenge of the key change in Ellington's "Sophisticated Lady." He assigned the passage to the oboeist, snorting: "He warned me he was a musical illiterate, but this is ridiculous!"

Prince Philip told me: "We don't do this job for the fun of it."

Prince Charles cautioned me at a state dinner: "If you wear your medal on such a long ribbon you'll get it in your soup." He said it happened to him once when he swung around to address his dinner companion, spraying a barebacked lady at a nearby table, whereupon she let out a yelp so loud that the Queen resolved never to invite her to a royal function again. Ever since, said His Royal Highness, he has worn his neck medals on short ribbons.

I dreamed, when both of us were much younger, that I was in a love scene with the Queen. It was based on the hayrick scene from the movie *The Red Shoes*, played by Moira Shearer and Marius Goring, and considered hot stuff at the time. My dream turned out great, but I felt guilty for months after.

I got a rejection slip from a publisher to whom I had sent my sexy war novel, saying: "This manuscript is very neatly typed."

Tales from the Press Club Bar

It was publisher Mel Hurtig who suggested a volume made up largely of the kind of stories press people tell one another. Nothing gets an author's attention more quickly than a publisher suggesting a book, especially if the last one worked. Hurtig had sat a couple of nights in Ottawa with political insiders and when he got back to Edmonton, his eyes aglow, he wrote saying that if some of those yarns could be put down on paper we would sell more books than Jean Chrétien, Ken Dryden, or anything ever published except his own *Canadian Encyclopedia*.

You have to have respect for Hurtig when you've written him one big money earner and he doesn't even send you a letter with your first fat royalty cheque. Booksellers love him, partly because he was once one himself, and partly because he sends them saleable books, without what I would call hype. No televised launchings, no celebrity parties, no skywriting, not even local reps to show you around during the book tour. I finally twisted his arm and said there was no way I could keep fifteen appointments in big TO in one day by riding the streetcars.

After the book had sold almost 50,000 copies there was still no sign of any money. Mel was anxious to dispose of some cartons of books he had in the warehouse, and he wanted to remainder them, over my protests that people were looking for copies. He won, as usual, and they went to Coles for 99 cents each, just after I had paid the author's discount price of $10 a copy to buy twenty-four books for my archives. You couldn't find a trace of that book today, for love or money.

Because of standard contract procedures, it was nine months after the Christmas rush, the only time Canadians buy Canadian books, before I saw any dough. When Hurtig said the cheque was being made up, I started watching the mail with special interest. Nothing came, and when I called he said the computer was down. Finally, he announced the money was on its way, so I resumed my vigil. Press people get a lot of junk mail, and I had developed the dangerous habit of discarding brown envelopes without opening them, glancing only at the letterhead on the outside. You get so you can smell a press release from twenty paces, and this particular day I threw away about fifteen of them, and sighed when there was nothing from my publisher. Then some small voice told me that one of those brown envelopes I had cast aside had no marking on it at all, itself suspicious. I dug back into the big wastebasket and sorted out the unmarked piece, noting that the postage meter stamp bore the slogan "Read the Canadian Encyclopedia." My own name and address were of the mailing machine variety, so I assumed Hurtig had sent me a news release, which wasn't exactly what I was looking for. I had the well-founded suspicion that even though I was one of Hurtig's favourite authors, my name would not be included among the entries in the encyclopedia. Neither, as it turned out, was his.

I ripped open the envelope and out fell a slip of paper, a computer printout from a printer that was low on ink. Holding the paper up to the light, I saw that it was a statement of my account with Hurtig, detailing the number of copies sold and my percentage, but the bottom line was so faint I couldn't read it. Peering into the envelope, I saw in its far recesses another piece of paper, and, upon retrieving it, observed that it was a cheque for $71,000.

I put aside thoughts that Hurtig had done this on purpose, knowing I would throw the envelope away. Why no covering letter? Why no registered mail? Why no bands playing, and angels chorusing? I hotfooted it to the bank, put the money in, and phoned Hurtig to tell him his plot had failed. What plot? He pleaded innocence as only Hurtig can, instantly switching the feeling of guilt to my shoulders, as only a publisher can do when dealing with an author.

So here was Hurtig with an idea for another book, a second volume of memoirs, even though I had told him I had high-graded my life for the first book, had only lived once, and had shot my best stories. "Steal some," he counselled — and hence this volume.

I warned him that most Press Club stories were actionable, but he said we could change the names. My second warning was not so easily disposed of, because it came true. Press Club people, I said, like to keep their stories to themselves, when it comes to print.

Jean Chrétien, for instance, had promised me an afternoon of recollections, but after the success of his own first book he was saving his best stuff for his own volume 2, and I couldn't have any. It was only by appealing to his sense of fair play, and recalling how I had boosted him for leader above all others, that he agreed to let me have one of his yarns.

Mike Duffy clammed up entirely, after all that we had meant to each other — he nominated me for president of the Press Gallery one year and, after I had won, moved my impeachment. This sort of bond should mean something, but Duffy said he wanted to keep all his stories intact so he could use them in his own book.

An even worse reaction came from Val Sears of the *Toronto Star*, who had the distinction in my first volume of being mentioned in the index though there was no mention of him in the book itself. This was because Sears had said he only reviewed books in which his name appeared in the index, so I obliged. This time, Sears delivered a diatribe about my nerve in seeking to use other people's stories in a book out of which I stood to make money. He said he wouldn't play unless I gave him at least the usual fees paid by the CBC for a freelance commentary, the moonlight variety of which Press Club and Press Gallery members dream.

This was serious, because Sears was one of the people Hurtig had sat with on that fateful evening in Ottawa when he conceived this book, and without Sears I couldn't hope for the flavour Hurtig would want. Sears, you should know, is a curmudgeon of the Edwardian school, a man as gracious in manner and dress as he is vicious in tongue. A few Searsian anecdotes would spice up the work and cause writings in high places. Besides, said Sears, the Press Club is always full of lobbyists and public relations people who have nothing of interest to say since they are listeners rather than talkers. Everybody's on the take, and nobody gives. Fortunately for me and readers of this book, I was able to overcome the objections and possessiveness of most of the stalwarts of the Press Club bar.

Why are press clubs still called press clubs and not media clubs? And why is our guiding principle, and refuge, still Freedom of the Press? Media has taken over from press in every other context, because broadcasters don't use presses and PR people have little to do with news. Without PR people, the National Press Club, and every other press club in the country, would fold; PR people pay higher fees and stand more rounds of drinks, and often put subsidies from their employers into the sagging club coffers. Yet I think the word media should not replace the ancient "press" in this context. Tales from the Media Club Bar doesn't have that ring of romance and mystery to it, conjuring up visions of trenchcoats and reputations made and broken, chandeliers ripped from their moorings, fisticuffs in the elevators, and holes driven in the walls. These things really happen in the National Press Club. We have the scars to prove it.

The Press Club is a place where women use the big F word, the big S word, and the wee P word, and where men tell dirty stories. Women in press clubs tend to talk rough and look at you with beady eyes, whereas press club men don't cuss much any more, leaving that to the sisterhood. And the women don't tell dirty stories, though they tend to laugh at the ones the men tell. Everyone talks shop, which for public relations people means office politics, for news people means federal politics, and for all people means gossip. Occasionally, people outside the media circle get in and listen, bemused. It's hard to be outside the media circle these days because the circle is so wide, covering not only people who are in the business but also people who would like to be, which includes just about everybody.

Seriously, yes, just about everybody.

Media work is not only more fun than any other kind of work, it's also more interesting, since it involves being paid to go places and see things that everybody else has to pay to go and see. It is a lifetime freeload, at the owners' expense, made respectable by the fact that we publish accounts of the things we see and hear, that the public may know our views and sometimes even the news. Indeed, as we keep saying, the public has a right to know, thus giving us the only excuse we need — Freedom of the Press.

There have been some epic battles at the club, one of the most memorable being that to admit women, twenty years ago. My own contribution to that successful fight was an impassioned speech in which I said if we admitted women to the oldest profession, I didn't see why they couldn't come into the second oldest. Especially, I added, since our profession had more lay experts than the oldest. Stirring stuff it was at the time, marking my place as an early feminist, though my mate keeps scoffing that I favoured women for all the wrong reasons.

To be truthful, though, the Press Club is a place I'm inclined to shun, because every time I go in there I either get the club bore, or somebody who wants to tell me what an asshole I am. Sometimes it's the club bore who tells me that; other times I suspect I myself am turning into the club bore, in addition to being an asshole.

Press clubs exist as places to drink, having no other function except the fraternal one. Legion halls used to be this way between the wars, before the Legion found religion and started calling itself a service club. Nobody ever called a press club a service club. Nobody ever will. Press clubs are places where dark deeds are plotted, and sometimes done.

The National Press Club has been called the most likely place to get laid, whether you be man, woman, or both, or neither. I have never heard of anybody getting laid there, though ample evidence exists that liaisons commenced at the second-floor bar have been brought to climax in the sixth-floor lounge, which isn't part of the Press Club at all, but rather an adjunct of the Parliamentary Press Gallery, with leather sofas. It used to have a grand piano until beer spills warped it into uselessness.

The Press Gallery, mind you, is not the Press Club. The Press Gallery is a body of professionals dedicated to the task of reporting on Parliament, government, mandarins and bureaucrats, lobbyists, foreign affairs outgoing and incoming, the economy, ecology, trade figures, and where to eat in Ottawa. The Press Gallery describes itself as the bridge between Parliament and the people, a role unrecognized either by Parliament or the people. It has a room on The Hill, in the Centre Block, together with a lounge with a fireplace, where freelancers and broadcasters live and work rent free. Members have the right to take notes in the House of Commons, a right seldom exercised these days because debates are ignored and most members choose to cover Question Period by TV or in their own re-enactments in the media mob scene that follows, in the foyer outside the doors of the House of Commons. It's called scrumming, but Trudeau used to call it scumming, and senior members of the Gallery call it slumming. As Fred Ennis of Newsradio put it, haughtily, "I don't do scrums."

Trouble is, the politicians have to do them, which is why so many of our best people don't go into politics.

The Gallery belongs overpoweringly to the electronic media, though the motto above the fireplace still says: "But a small drop of ink, falling like dew upon a thought, produces that which makes thousands, perhaps millions, think." Nothing is said about what happens when the lights, cameras, and microphones alight en masse atop a thought, perhaps because the idea is too horrible to contemplate.

Politicians come to hate the Press Gallery, and all prime ministers, including Mulroney, have loathed it. Many develop an affection for the Press Club, partly because MPs get complimentary memberships and the drinks and meals are cheaper than on The Hill, now that the freeload there has been eliminated and the quality of food in the Parliamentary Restaurant has gone down.

Most members of the Press Gallery belong to the Press Club, though they regard it as slumming. The Press Gallery is supposed to be the summit of the news business in Canada, but hardly anyone outside Ottawa regards it as such. Press Gallery people tend to be earnest and there aren't many jokes there now; there used to be in times when members took themselves less seriously. With concentration of media ownership, just about everybody in the Gallery is a member of one corporate team or another. You don't get, as once happened, the bureau chief of the Canadian Press jamming the bureau chief of British United Press into a phone booth, ramming the door shut with a chair, and setting the booth on fire. The CP man, Clyde Blackburn, sat watching his opponent roast, humming "Can It Be True, Someone Like You Could Love Me?"

The BUP man, Norman MacLeod, sought revenge when the two of them were on assignment in San Francisco and MacLeod had a room directly below Blackburn in the Mark Hopkins. MacLeod visited Blackburn's room and, while his host was in the can, opened the French windows and placed Blackburn's telephone far out on the ledge. Then he went to his room below and phoned Blackburn's room, sitting by his open window to watch Blackburn's body hurtle past. But Blackburn, on hearing his phone, fell on his hands and knees and groped for the instrument in the darkness. He crawled to the doors, fumbled outside along the ledge until he found the phone, picked it up and snarled: "Missed me, you bastard."

A reviewer of my earlier memoir said it was weakened by inclusion of stories more suited to telling in the Press Club bar, but it seemed notable to me that these were the stories readers liked best. Hence a second volume replete with the kind of things media people talk about, most of them with the funny side out.

Maniacs of Canada, Arise!

Canadians have no heroes but occasionally go into a tizzy over political leaders, for reasons that have little to do with politics. These manifestations are called manias, and they have been likened to the tulip mania in medieval Holland, or the South Sea Bubble fever that swept Britain into madness. This particular madness coincided with the invention of gin, which paralysed the British, mind and body, for sixty years.

Canadians concentrate on their politics only at election time — betweentimes they tend to doze off, living up to their reputation as the most politically illiterate people in the Western world. It was thus that the country became the most socialized land in the Western world, without anybody understanding how it happened, or why, or even when. Then again, it may have been the gin.

The first mania of modern times occurred in 1958, when a majority of Canadians came to the conclusion that John Diefenbaker was our version of the Second Coming, a view shared by Diefenbaker himself. Some people hold that illusion to this day, but most were disillusioned and resolved never to abandon themselves to such an orgy again.

Ten years later, the population flipped for Pierre Elliott Trudeau. Women became stupefied and droopy lipped in his presence, the phenomenon affecting the young, the middle aged, and the old in equal measure. Kissing and swooning were much in evidence, and to judge by the sobs and sighs there was a good deal of coming, though not of the second kind. And when it was over, most people were disillusioned and resolved never to abandon themselves to such an orgy again.

The strange thing is, they didn't.

A man and woman came among them to win the greatest political victory in the history of the nation, bigger than Diefenbaker in 1958, bigger than Trudeau in 1968, but without mania. Brian and Mila Mulroney had the stuff of mania in them, for they were a handsome couple, skilled in many languages, with a beguiling set of kids, and style to burn. Mulroney showed himself to be a master politician by unseating Joe Clark as Tory leader at a time when Clark was ahead in the public-opinion polls. It was a case of substituting a massive chin for Joe's receding one. After splitting the Tory Party wide open, Mulroney sewed it back together again with surgical skill, by offering all the top jobs to the people he had just blown away.

This signalled the stuff of greatness, and in the campaign of 1984 we waited for the inevitable mania to set in. But it didn't. People cheered Mila but they stayed cool about Mulroo, as we came to call him, in expectation of Mulroomania. When the votes were counted it was all there for him, except the emotion. So the pundits said it wasn't so much a landslide for Mulroney as it was a rejection of the Liberals. People were weary of Trudeau and all his works, and they took it out on his successor, John Turner, who seemed no more likely to cause a mania than Robert Stanfield had been.

Had the Canadian people, at last, become mania-proof? Or, having fallen for Diefenbaker's folksy Westernness, and Trudeau's sexy Frenchness, were they impervious to Irish blarney, the more so because the modern Irish tend to smithereens rather than smiles?

Most of the time you couldn't hear what Mulroney was saying, he spoke so softly. It was like a tuba trying to play the melody, except when he burst into song, in which case an acceptable Irish tenor came out of his narrow lips. He always sang "When Irish Eyes are Smiling" in public, though in private he displayed a knowledge of the words of just about every song written between 1920 and 1939. His duet with Ronald Reagan in Quebec City was unforgettable, though Reagan seemed to forget it faster than anybody else, if indeed he ever memorized it at all. And nobody who saw it will ever forget the night in the National Press Club when the gang gathered around the piano and, to his tormentor Shrieky Sheila Copps of the Liberal Rat Pack, he sang: "You Made Me Love You, I Didn't Want To Do It!" With feeling, and Copps was bugeyed.

But no mania — meaning the nation has passed eighteen years without one, making us eight years overdue if these things are supposed to strike every decade, the way it used to be with wars. Trudeau stayed around too long, because of Stanfield and Clark, who were unable to generate manias of their own. No matter, there will be enough manias in the future, and if they aren't centred on people, perhaps they will generate around issues, such as free trade, the deficit, the value of the dollar, or the prospect of Prince Charles ascending the throne. Some future Diefenbaker may be among us even now, waiting to unleash his or her wattles; or some Trudeau, pocked and flinty-eyed, tight-trousered and open-shirted, sandalled and buckskin-jacketed, doing triples on his or her flying trapeze.

Until then, it's Tory time, exciting only when Mulroney raises his voice to Broadbent pitch and puts aside the bedroom tones that his Venus de Mila alone appreciates. The rest of us have to write about issues, and it's heavy going watching the Americans and the British and the Russians having all the fun, mania-wise. Eh?

Messing with Mulroo

When I asked Brian Mulroney to talk about funny ways to run the country, he wound up telling me what a funny country this is to run. Things change so fast, he said, and he wasn't complaining about his rough days in office so much as holding out the prospect of better days to come, putting his government in great shape for re-election in 1988 or 1989.

I noted that the government had been in power for only a few months when media reports said the government was "on the ropes." And at the start of the second year in office, the media theme was that the government faced "its last chance."

Said the Prime Minister: "Y'know, to put it in perspective, three years ago I was running the Iron Ore Company of Canada."

Yes, I agreed, and the same thing had been true with Pierre Trudeau — three years after supporting the NDP against the Liberals he was the Liberal prime minister of Canada.

"Absolutely," said Mulroney. "Here we are sitting in the Langevin Block. In that time, I became leader of the Conservative Party, got elected in Central Nova, and sat in the House of Commons as leader of the opposition. Trudeau resigned on me — he was kind enough to resign — and Turner came in, and he pulled the plug, since he was leading by fourteen points in the polls, and we came in and formed a government. All those things in less than three years.

"So here we are. We're not going to have an election for three years, and these people down the street are talking about last chance, we've got to do something tomorrow! Imagine what's going to happen to us in our lives, in three years. The day we go to the country, Canada won't be at all what it is today. The problems that we're talking about will have no relevance to the issues, in late 1988 or 1989. But there it is."

I had gone to the PM in quest of anecdotes, because he had been involved in some of the strangest episodes in the history of the Tory Party and of the country. In some of them he was the central figure, notably his unsuccessful quest for the party leadership in 1976 and his successful run in 1983. He went after the mantle of Joe Clark, who was leading the public-opinion polls at the time.

Mulroney was not disposed to wash Tory dirty linen in public, which in itself makes him an unusual Conservative prime minister. But he was ready to tell stories on himself, which puts him in step with both John Diefenbaker and Joe Clark, and utterly out of step with Pierre Trudeau, who never told a joke in his life, let alone one in which the laugh was on him.

"Here's one that actually happened," said Mulroney, with that conspiratorial "listen" he uses when he's warming up, the way a lot of Quebec English-speakers do.

"It's funny what you remember. I was part of the welcoming crowd when Diefenbaker came back from the Commonwealth Conference where he made his famous speech about a candle in the window for South Africa, after she was kicked out. There was a Conservative meeting in Ottawa at the time, 1960 or 1961, and there were snowbanks, so it must have been March. We organized this huge, tumultuous welcome back to the Chief for his magnificent role in the Commonwealth. I remember how he enjoyed the adulation of the hundreds and hundreds of Conservatives at the airport that day.

"Well, when I came back from the Commonwealth Conference after a not-unsuccessful first appearance in Nassau and I got off the plane, apart from the press on the right-hand side there was one person, George Hees. Hees! So, in gratitude, I came down and went over to George, in part to convey the impression to the press that Hees was the official greeter. I said to him, 'God, George, I want to thank you for coming out to the airport to welcome me home.'

"George says, 'Well, actually, Brian, I'm here to borrow your plane. I'm going home for the weekend, and this will get me to Trenton.'

"I had to laugh, and I thought of Old Dief. Can you imagine Dief, if he'd come back and there'd been George as the one person to meet him?"

The hated Hees, one of "them," one of Diefenbaker's names that would live in infamy, returned to the fold and now the last active cabinet remnant of the Diefenbaker glory years.

Mulroney's story about nobody waving hello recalls a similar fate that befell Diefenbaker five years before he became prime minister, when he was travelling around the country in near anonymity, trying with half his strength to whip up support for a leader he despised, George Drew.

In the 1953 campaign, Diefenbaker was the only passenger on a Maritime Central Airways flight into New Glasgow, Nova Scotia, a city that would take its place, thirty years later, as one of Brian Mulroney's many home towns. The flight attendant had no idea who Diefenbaker was, and she was startled to see a crowd waiting at the small terminal, rounded up by the local candidate to greet the visiting speaker. "Some distinguished person must have missed this flight," she said to Diefenbaker. "They're going to get a heck of a shock when they see you're the only person getting off!"

Ten years later Mike Pearson suffered a similar comedown on his way to the 1963 election victory, when he attended a rally in the Toronto York West riding of Liberal MP Red Kelly, the hockey Hall of Famer who was then a forward with the Toronto Maple Leafs. An embarrassed Kelly was kept busy signing autographs while the future prime minister stood by like an off-season hockey coach. Kelly pleaded with somebody to want Pearson's autograph, but he stopped when a freckle-faced youngster asked: "Who does he play for?"

I egged Mulroney on — any topic "in your long and spectacular involvement with the Conservative Party."

"There was one that happened in 1976 during the leadership campaign," said Mulroney, after a long pause while he racked his brain. "I came down in the elevator at the Skyline Hotel, and there was nobody in the lobby. We were on our way to a policy session, and over against the wall there was one fellow, with a T-shirt on, and wearing a Pat Nowlan badge. I assumed he was a delegate, and I needed every vote I could get, so I went over to say hello. He had a bottle of Tuborg in his hand. I introduced myself: 'I'm Brian Mulroney.'

"He said: 'I know.'

"I said: 'Well. Thank you.'

"He just looked at me. So I turned around and started to walk away, when he asked: 'Mr. Mulroney, can I tell you something?'

"I said 'Sure, I'd be grateful.'

"And he replied: 'You're the biggest horse's ass I've ever met in my life.'

"Michel Cogger was with me — you know, Michel who was described at the time as looking like Claude Ruel in a $400 suit. Squat. Well, Michel laughed and said: 'It's okay — don't worry about a thing. I've got him down as undecided!'"

The day after telling me this story, Mulroney appointed Cogger to the Senate. Our talk must have triggered his memory. I asked Mulroney if he had any comment on the most widely quoted thing said about him, Mrs. Mulroney's revelation that he changed many of the baby's diapers because he had no sense of smell.

"In point of fact," he replied, "it's exactly true. I have an obstruction right here in the upper part of my nose, and it would need quite an operation. It's a massive obstruction of the nasal passage. It does affect breathing, and every so often I have to do this." And he gave a deep sniff. "That's to relieve the pressure," he said. "There could be all kinds of baby's activity going on right in my lap, you know, and until it hit my trousers I wouldn't have the foggiest idea of what was going on."

I remarked it was an interesting and intimate glimpse of what goes on in high places, and that people eat it up, as they do all the stuff in the political gossip columns.

"You can't tell what will come out, or how it will be perceived," said Mulroney. "You can't blame people for being interested, but I see some of this stuff that is just absolutely false, total fabrication. I suppose there's nothing you can do."

I reminded him of what Trudeau went through at the time of

his marriage breakup, and what Joe Clark went through when he was being pilloried in the public press. Trudeau's performance under media pressure was the more remarkable, I suggested, because he hated failure, and here he was with his marriage failing utterly, and he didn't flinch in public.

Mulroney agreed that the international press coverage of the Trudeau breakup was "really quite awful," adding: "I thought that was the time when Trudeau probably conducted himself with the greatest dignity possible."

And yet, I said, I always doubted that Trudeau deserved full marks because Margaret took the whole brunt of public criticism, and that didn't seem fair because obviously he was a hell of a guy to have to live with.

"Well," mused Mulroney, "that would be my appraisal from sitting there in Montreal and watching this unfold — I would have given him the highest possible marks. I didn't know Margaret at the time, I didn't know any of the details, but I suppose you're right."

"About media being selective? That's our greatest power — if we don't report something, it hasn't happened."

Mulroney agreed with that, and with my suggestion that it applied to coverage of Parliament, where the debates go unreported and hence have no public impact.

"Well, take this," said Mulroney, nodding his head. "I went into the House during one noon hour to find out how the debate was going on our reform of Parliament, and I offered to speak. Jim McGrath said for me to do it right that minute, so I got to my feet and spoke for fifteen minutes off the cuff on reform. Nobody reported it, to this day, and if I may say so, it was a pretty good speech. Not a single word has been mentioned about it. It confirms exactly what you've just said about selection, and about nobody covering Parliament, except for the forty-five minutes of Question Period, which is theatrics.

"That's what parliamentary democracy is in the process of being reduced to, and that's why I've supported this parliamentary reform so much. If we don't do something to elevate our members of Parliament and give them the capacity to make decisions and start running roughshod over the bureaucrats, as opposed to the other way around — and I mean that in the best sense of the word — we're in trouble."

I suggested this would cause him trouble enough, if party discipline were cut back and his caucus so big.

"I know," said Mulroney, "I'm going to be the most embarrassed guy in town. I'll be so busy wiping the egg off my face — but if that's the price you pay for an exciting deputation of people smart enough to make up their own minds from time to time against you, then that is a reasonable price to make Parliament what it should be."

From Mulroney's office on the third floor of the Langevin Block, across the street from Parliament Hill, I drifted down to the ground floor and the office of Bill Fox, the PM's communications director and the only man who still calls me "Chief" from our days together at Southam News. With him was the prime minister's press secretary, Michel Gratton, one-time rock singer, political columnist, and one of the best political satirists in the business, in both maternal languages.

Fox and Gratton have been called the twins from Appalachia, because they look like a couple of rogues just in from the latest Mafia convention. When they appear in news photos with Mulroney the impression is that the PM has been taken hostage. Actually, they have an abiding interest in his safety, and when people complain about the security, they tell you about Olof Palme being shot dead on a Stockholm street.

Not as many people seem to want to kill Mulroney as used to want to shoot Trudeau, but the risk is rated high. The Mounties are the ones who tell the prime minister where to go, and when, and how, outside the Parliament Buildings. Inside the buildings, the House of Commons security officers take over, fully armed. If any prime minister from Sir John A. to Mike Pearson were to return to The Hill, the security measures would be the thing that would surprise them most of all.

It was the collapse of those arrangements that gave Fox and Gratton their most memorable funny story. *Over to Gratton:*

We were coming away from the prime minister's office on the third floor of the Centre Block, and we got to the West Door where the limousine was supposed to be waiting to take the PM home for lunch. I went through the door and saw there was no limo. No motorcade, no Mounties, no nothing.

Fox followed me and went right around in the revolving door and back inside, where the boss was standing talking to some people. And Fox said: "Straight out. My office." Meaning, make a run for it.

We were being followed by cameras and reporters who wanted a scrum. The boss instinctively figured there was something wrong so when Fox and I led, he followed, and we started hoofing it down The Hill looking for a place to hide.

Well, there was a lady tourist with a baby, and he stopped to say hello. Then, Ambassador Lloyd Francis had to be greeted. On we went, with the media pack in hot pursuit, and still no cops. We crossed Wellington Street and were right into my office on the ground floor here before the boss said anything, and what he said was: "Where's the limo? You got it in the washroom?" So he sat down, and all of a sudden some dodo with a walkie-talkie peeked in and this guy bellowed into his blower: "We've found him!" And then they said they've got the limo at the door, so we looked out the window and it wasn't there. Finally, it showed up.

And the next day when you picked up your Ottawa *Citizen* there was a colour picture on the front page of the prime minister, Gratton, and Fox, and a piece about this dramatic break from the past, the PM out among the people, none of this old Liberal security guard crap!

I pressed Gratton for a Quebec story, saying that otherwise I was going to have a completely Anglo book and my mate, the Honourable Member for Gatineau, would kick the bejesus out of me.

"Well," said Fox, "speaking of herself, what about the last day of the 1984 election campaign, when Mulroney's last stop, at 11 o'clock at night, was to bring the Boeing 727 into Gatineau airport, the biggest plane to land there, before or since?"

Fox called it the most extraordinary day of the campaign, because the flight started in Montreal, then stopped in Toronto, London, and Thunder Bay, then Mulroney went to North Bay and Mrs. Mulroney went to The Soo, then they went to Kenora, and finally a stop in Gatineau before finishing in Mont Joli. "By the time we landed in Gatineau, if you had shouted to the boys at the back for a dateline, you'd have got four different answers."

I was there that night. There were 1200 people at that airport, and if Mulroney had descended on a moonbeam they couldn't have been more impressed. There was the candidate on the tarmac with the only other person who thought she could win, and the plane looked as big as a Jumbo, and, though nobody wrote about it, it was my most memorable moment of the campaign. It must have swung some votes, though some of Mulroney's handlers deemed it a waste of his time. The riding went Tory for the first time in its long history, back to the days when Sir Wilfrid Laurier held the seat.

My Hobbyhorses Always Lose

Almost no cause that I have espoused has ever prospered, which tells you something about the power of the pundit in our society. Bruce Hutchison once wrote that the first requirement of a columnist is to be read, and I'm not sure there is much after that. My own philosophy is to entertain, and slip readers mickeys of information without their knowing, the way you hide the pill in the dogfood.

I battled for recognition of the People's Republic of China for eleven years before it came to pass — lamenting the reticence of the Diefenbaker and Pearson governments, and cheering Trudeau when he finally did it.

My own visit to China in 1965 was something of a trailblazer for Western journalists and resulted in a book in the same vein as Trudeau's *Two Innocents in Red China*. I included, among other things, a list of the top forty hit songs with the comrades of the time: In Years of Misery, Song of the Anyuan Railway and Mine Workers Club, Workers Peasants and Soldiers Unite, The Martyr's Song, Joining Forces of Chinghang Mountain, Down with the Local Bullies and Distribute the Land, Seizing a Strong Point, Go to the Rear of the Enemy, Who's Afraid of Being Jailed, Millions of Serfs Stand Up, Socialism is Good, Chairman Mao is Our Captain, We Must Liberate our Territory Taiwan, Commune Members are Sunflowers, Learn from the Ta Chai Production Brigade, and so on.

In the last chapter of that book I expressed admiration for China's self-help spirit but predicted that human greed would assert itself, as it tends to do everywhere. Chairman Mao had the same idea, because he sprung the Cultural Revolution once I was out of the country. As soon as that madness was over, Canada recognized China and I went back in 1975 to see how things were going, only to find the country in the thrall of the Gang of Four, a revolutionary government even tougher than the one before.

My admiration for the Chinese people was undiminished, though I continued to fear that individual ambition would assert itself and undo all Chairman Mao's dreams and plans for his country. Everything that has followed has tended to bear out that prophecy. The revolution of rising expectations bodes no good for China, whose governors are going to need all the sympathy and help they can get from the rest of us. The Chinese people are being taught to want our way of life, and they can't have it, because there are too many of them and their assigned portion of the world's land mass is too poor.

It was a pleasure to have associated with them and moved among them, making friends with my companion and interpreter Mr. An, who shared many jokes, including his tendency to mix the words "concubine" and "cucumber." In the 1980s Mr. An came to Ottawa as interpreter for a series of Chinese ambassadors. We met after his arrival, embraced heartily, and swore eternal friendship. We lunched together once and never saw each other again except across the room at receptions. After six years in Ottawa he returned to China without saying goodbye.

So much for my support for that successful cause. All else amounts to sound and fury, signifying nothing.

The status of the Crown has gone down since I took up the cudgels for it, but this is an ongoing cause not yet lost.

My 1960's advocacy of Canada's withdrawal from the NATO alliance in return for Poland's leaving the Warsaw Pact got me a dinner at the Polish Embassy and an encouraging word from Mike Pearson when he was leader of the opposition. Nothing more was heard of it and we adopted nuclear arms instead.

I cheered Pierre Trudeau's proposal for patriation of the

constitution and insertion of a Charter of Rights, but when he actually did it he had to make so many compromises that, as he himself admitted, it resembled a make-work project for lawyers. What we didn't envisage at the time was that he himself would be one of the lawyers.

My promotion of Ottawa as one of the most beautiful capital cities in the world keeps drawing scorn from other parts of the country, especially from people who have never visited the place and seen their taxes at work. Media critics of Ottawa will pass away, but the city will endure, encased in glass that ensures that if the place is ever nuked, everything will melt into a great crystalline lump that should baffle future generations — if there are any.

Douglas Fullerton, who conceived the Rideau Canal skating rink in Ottawa, should be named an honorary Father of Confederation and given the Order of the Achilles Tendon. He also did the ski trails and bicycle paths that ring the scenic areas of the capital, so in a primitive way he was to Ottawa what Christopher Wren was to London.

Fullerton is a man who made his dreams into reality, so let me digress for a moment to talk about him. The thing most people remember when they think of Fullerton is his spectacular stammer, one of the great speech impediments in the history of public life, known to keep audiences on the edge of their chairs for hours on end.

My most memorable exposure to Fullerton at the podium came at a celebration of the fiftieth anniversary of that great Hull restaurant, Madame Burgers, for years the only fit place to eat in Ottawa. The Madame herself was the guest of honour, and the celebrants were picked by her from her most treasured patrons through the years. I hadn't spent all that much time there but was glad to be in the crowd, and everybody present got to make a little speech about what Madame Burgers, and the Madame herself, had meant in their lives.

Everything went swimmingly until it came Fullerton's turn. He got to the podium and started to crank himself up, which was something like the count-down to a space-shuttle launch, though the shuttle had not then been devised. Finally, Fullerton hit the right groove and was off in an eloquent outburst when, at a table directly in front of the podium, a senior member of the Quebec bench was seized with an attack of vertigo and threw up in the most spectacular manner, spraying his table mates and falling, face forward, into the goo. Everybody in the room gasped with horror. All eyes were on the stricken judge and his companions, who leaped to his assistance and proceeded to remove him from the room, while others got on with the mopping up, assisted by the waiters.

My own eyes, through all this, were on Fullerton. When the judge barfed, Fullerton stopped speaking and a look of dismay came over his face. I saw his lips move and caught what he was saying. It was: "Sh!" And as the drama developed, he kept saying that same syllable, over and over: "Sh...Sh...Sh... Sh!" He shook his head, and he blinked his eyes, and he watched while they lifted the judge and carried him away, with the mopup brigade doing its stuff, and a new cloth being set for the table. "Sh...Sh...Sh...Sh..." And finally, in a paroxysm of frustration: "Oh......Sh...Sh...Sh...SHIT!"

There followed a few moments of calm, during which order was restored in the audience. Fullerton was able to resume, back at the bottom of the speech barrel, meaning he had to wind himself up again, which he did, and he made the finest speech of the night.

Another windmill against which I have tilted has been the movement to establish professional standards in the news business. We're no closer to it than we were when I started fifty years ago, and some think we've lost ground, with any pretence at factual reporting abandoned in a wash of punditry. No credential is needed to enter the news business, and none to start a newspaper, buy one, close one, merge a couple, or fire everybody on the staff, though the trade unions have made that a bit tougher. The punditry segment of the business is open to anybody with the nerve to try, and no skills are necessary apart from the ability to attract attention and hold it for at least five minutes — one minute, on television.

Editors exert a measure of control by selection, and by deeming that any item of news, or column of opinion, is unfit for public consumption and throwing it out. There are no established qualifications for this job, either, though the Kent Royal Commission tried to propose some. But its recommendations were hounded into oblivion by the media people themselves, who preferred being in thrall to the owners than to any set of professional requirements imposed by law. This fear of government intervention in media, based on the assumption that government money is tainted, always seems to beg the question of the CBC, supported as it is, in its news operations, entirely by funds voted by Parliament.

I have opposed the principle of compulsory retirement at age sixty-five, and am devoting my terminal years to the cause, though it is too late to save me from being put out to pasture by the decree of some unseen actuary in some company pension-fund office. It is a form of capital punishment, and hence irreversible. This fight may be won because of Trudeau's charter and its ban on discrimination based on age. Also, today's young people fear that the overburden of seniors in society will soon become too costly to be borne, unless the seniors are kept in useful, productive employment.

I urged reform of the Senate, but Mike Pearson pointed out that the last thing any prime minister would want to tolerate was a Senate with powers, the country being hard enough to govern as things were. So I advocated abolition of the Senate, but Brian Mulroney observed that no prime minister could live without it, as a place to dump people, and that when John Crosbie advocated abolition "that just proves he's not prime minister."

The Senate scuppered me on a couple of occasions in Moscow and Peking when I was defending our system of government, while making clear I was not urging it on the Russians or the Chinese, who had problems enough. I was explaining how much stock we put in the fact that our people could vote freely in elections, though my Communist colleagues were puzzled about why, when these elections were won, we in media then fell upon the victors and proceeded on the assumption that they were rogues and scoundrels who needed to be impeached. The answer was the invigorating aspect of cut and thrust, and the claim that our constant confrontations kept everybody awake and honest. My listeners seemed unimpressed, but they didn't actually start laughing until I got to explaining the workings of our Senate and how its members are chosen.

Here's a tip: If you ever get into an argument with a Communist over the merits of our respective systems of government, don't try to explain the Canadian Senate. Just say it's a place of honour for our respected sages. It isn't, of course, but that's the only explanation that makes the slightest sense. And you'll get nowhere trying to explain what party bagmen are.

One of my most vigorous fights was against the unification of the armed forces, and the then minister of national defence, Paul Hellyer, mopped the floor with me and a passel of admirals and generals who fought for separate service identities. The great experiment went ahead and was a failure on almost every count, though it didn't matter all that much because our peacetime armed forces became too expensive to maintain in fighting trim, and we persuaded ourselves that fighting trim didn't mean much anyway in the nuclear balance of terror.

Eventually, the wheel came full circle and Robert Coates restored the separate uniforms, just before he had to leave the defence portfolio for visiting a strip club near our NATO casern in Lahr, West Germany. If the unification of our armed forces didn't puzzle our friends and foes, the firing of Coates for going to a sex joint confused them utterly.

The ultimate nonsense was to order our navy into Arctic waters with ships built for cruising in the Caribbean. And when the Americans sent an icebreaker through our Arctic waters we resolved to build a bigger breaker, though it wasn't clear just what ice it would be called upon to crush, or why.

I have fought against that great Canadian contribution to the democratic process, the federal-provincial conference. But the sessions keep getting bigger and bigger, with provincial premiers staking out more and more turf to the point where people stop talking about the Balkanization of Canada and refer instead to the Canadianization of the Balkans.

I have insisted that our immigrants leave their quarrels at home and accept our system of government as they find it, rather than bellyaching. My own Irish forebears didn't do a very good job of this, bringing the Orange and the Green dispute to our shores, where it raged for more than 100 years, though not as hotly as in the United States, which still sends money and guns to keep the Irish troubles going. By the time Canadian Irish reached the third or fourth generation the fires of conflict seemed to die down, contributing greatly to peace and quiet in our midst, broken only by squabbles among new arrivals from other parts of Europe, the Middle East, the Caribbean, and Asia.

Canadians of Japanese origin have been making a fuss about reparations for outrages inflicted upon them during the Second World War. I was witness to those outrages and remember that they had the full support of the Canadian people at the time. We were at war with Japan, and that government decreed that once a Japanese always a Japanese. My latter-day suggestion about reparations was that at least part of the cost be paid by the government of Japan, since they started the hostilities and committed many atrocities on our soldiers. But neither our government nor the Japanese saw any merit in my proposal.

During the Quiet Revolution in Quebec I tried to contribute to the English-speaking side of the dialogue that everybody in Quebec said they wanted, but they interpreted my interventions as racism. When we sent Tim Creery to open the first Southam bureau in Quebec City, his French-speaking colleagues there dubbed him "frogman for the Lynch mob."

I have fought for the improvement of Canadian wine. Once, when a domestic variety of plonk was served at a banquet to celebrate the 150th birthday of Sir John A. Macdonald, I wrote that if Sir John had survived to taste this stuff, he might have felt that the country wasn't worth founding in the first place. The domestic wineries immediately cancelled all their advertising in our newspapers. Over the years, however, they have worked assiduously to improve their product and some of it today is quite potable. The problem is that in order to make better stuff they had to raise the price, to the point where good foreign wines are sometimes cheaper.

I have written that the automobiles of today are better than anything ever made by man, adding to life's joys as well as its sorrows, and certainly adding to its costs. I have argued the excellence of today's cars with critics up to and including Ralph Nader, and thought perhaps I had scored on him until I learned that his fee for the appearance was $20,000, to the $200 I was getting, and that he had two other appearances that day in other cities, at similar fees, travelling to them in his own jet.

I have argued for Canada's membership in the Organization of American States, feeling that Latin America, with all its shortcomings, offers more return for our attention than Africa, Asia, or any other part of the Third World. (Whatever happened to the Second World? We were once a leading member of it, but it disappeared and became the Developed World, which isn't the same thing at all, since it includes the United States and the Soviet Union.) But we never cared enough to join the OAS, and to this day Canadians seem less interested in tidings from Latin America than in news from Africa or Asia. I still think an exchange involving Latin women coming to Canada and Canadian women going to Latin America might pay great dividends to all, including the males of both regions.

I have fought the idea of Maritime Union, on the grounds that Prince Edward Islanders are a breed apart and New Brunswickers and Nova Scotians are separate races. Union isn't going to happen anyway because the biggest saving would be in cutting the public payroll, and the public payroll is the biggest industry in the Maritimes, the one thing that keeps the economy rolling, oiled as it is by injections of money from the federal treasury.

My own failures are dwarfed by some of the big ideas we had as a nation that never came to pass. Some of them remain dreams for the twenty-first century, which somebody is sure to say will belong to Canada.

Speaking of which, has it occurred to you that Sir Wilfrid Laurier's prediction about the twentieth century actually came true? Assuming he didn't mean for us to become a superpower, which would have represented disaster on a massive scale, everything else he might have had in mind has happened. Consider that we have the best of the American way of life, with none of the responsibilities, since the world doesn't give a damn what happens here. We are among the privileged of the world in terms of location and riches, with marvellous cities, the best-housed people on the globe, and the best fed, with food to spare for anybody in the world who will buy it or agree to share it with the hungry without theft.

At the time of writing we are just getting over such big problems as tainted tuna, caucus eavesdropping, missing messengers, lavish expense accounts, and lippy flight attendants. Ask anybody from any other country in the world and they will tell you that a country where these are the main problems of the day is the most fortunate country in the world, which is another way of saying that the twentieth century belongs to us. In the words of Pogo, we have seen the enemy, and the enemy is us, and we have triumphed.

Now, about the things we haven't done, that we ought to have. We start with a causeway across the Strait of Belle Isle, between Newfoundland and Labrador. This body of water is about fifteen kilometres wide, and unfortunately it is almost that same measurement from top to bottom, which would make a causeway, or a dam, difficult to build. But the benefits would be beyond calculation. Maybe the project has to wait until we really have some reason to be sore at Europe, because the immediate effects of the causeway, apart from enabling the people of Labrador to walk to Newfoundland (and vice versa), would be to divert the icy Labrador current across the Atlantic, converting Europe into an icecap, covered with seals. And the Gulf Stream would be drawn up into the Gulf of St. Lawrence, where its name tells us it rightfully belongs, and would convert that entire area into a tropical paradise. Imagine Prince Edward Island abloom with frangipanis amid the palm trees? And Newfoundland bursting with poinsettias and monkeys chattering amid the jungle vines? Orange groves on Anticosti, and gambling casinos in every cove?

Then there was the proposal to build a glass dome over the town of Frobisher Bay, making it an urban metropolis in the Arctic. They built the town, but not the dome, and the results are disappointing. Now, we couldn't afford it, even in the best of times, but it would have been cheaper than trying to put men on the moon, which doesn't seem to have led anywhere.

The townsite of Resolute was a similar disappointment, a monument to our northern dreams that nobody had the guts to fulfil, or the money. There remains an outfit called the Resolute Bay Yacht Club, which I have visited, and which is remarkable for the fact that the ice never goes out of the bay, so nobody ever gets to put to sea. This is just as well considering the fact that the place has the highest per capita consumption of booze in the nation, if not the world.

At one time we were going to bring in 30,000 Koreans to harness the Athabasca Tar Sands, but maybe it's just as well we didn't, considering conditions in Korea, not to mention Athabaska. We decided to drive imported Korean cars instead, which pleased everybody but our own carmakers.

Then there was the Prince Edward Island causeway, which would hook the island to the mainland and make it possible for mainlanders to visit the beaches and Green Gables without lining up for the ferry. It makes sense, but we'll never see it, even though causeways of greater length and complexity abound in other parts of the world. In the Florida Keys and across Lake Pontchartrain, just outside New Orleans, for example, you can drive many kilometres out of sight of land merely in quest of a crawfish dinner, which is delicious when you get to it.

There was a very sensible idea to build a canal system from Montreal up the Ottawa River, through Lake Nipissing, and down the French River into Lake Huron, but that got ditched in favour of the St. Lawrence Seaway, which hasn't been so big a hit though it seemed the answer to a lot of prayers at the time. Maritimers hated it because of lost business for their ports, and they put a hex on it which causes lock walls to fall down, bridges to collapse, and ships to sink in the channel from time to time.

And there was talk of a canal from the Lakehead across northern Ontario and the Prairies to Edmonton, following the route of the old voyageur fur traders. But again the dig never commenced, and never will, so we won't see giant ocean liners steaming through the flatlands.

The Chignecto Canal, across the isthmus that connects Nova Scotia to New Brunswick, should have been dug a hundred years ago, and parts of it were. But it never got finished, so Nova Scotia remains a peninsula rather than an island, which prevents it from drifting away and fulfilling the prophecy of its provincial song, "Farewell to Nova Scotia."

We did build the causeway across the Strait of Canso to Cape Breton Island, but a fat lot of good it did. That strait, like Belle Isle, was deep, and it took a whole mountain of rock to fill it. The project was managed, however, allowing commerce to flow freely to Cape Breton, when the whole economy of the island turned to dross, making it the biggest distress case in the country, bigger than Newfoundland. Every industry was closed or crippled, and no new ones showed up even though the government offered to put everything on the tab and provide free dancing girls.

There was talk about harnessing the Fundy tides, the greatest single energy source in the world, with power provided gratis by the moon. But instead of doing it we built a timid pilot project and, right there on the Fundy shore, with those mighty tides washing at their feet, we put two gigantic power stations, one oil fired, the other nuclear. At least the nuclear one worked, though there were eighty-five labour stoppages while it was being built. And the boilers they put in came from Ontario, cracked.

And what about the tunnel to Vancouver Island? Or the Mackenzie Valley pipeline, blocked to help the very natives who might have made a living building and running it?

Enough. We have the West Edmonton Mall, don't we? And Gretzky? Think of the Big O, the CN Tower, the cultural palaces across the country that have replaced the movie dream houses of the 1920s and 1930s. Think of all the good restaurants that have taken the place of the greasy spoons. Think of the universities and the hospitals and the high schools, even if we can't afford them, all paid for by plastic. So think of Visa and MasterCard and smile when you join the line-up to use the automatic teller machine. And notice how much more you see and hear of the French language than would have been the case when Laurier made his prediction.

Sir Wilfrid would be proud, n'est-ce pas? Eh?

Our Funniest Thing

The funniest thing about Canada is that it was founded by a bunch of lawyers scratching away with quill pens. It almost ended the same way, with lawyers using ballpoints. Instead, there was a new constitution signed in person by the Queen in the pouring rain, which caused the ink on her signature to smudge. A dissident later spattered the page with red ink. In Canadian terms that rated as an act of terrorism, which is why Canada is known as one of the most comical as well as the most fortunate countries in a world where good humour is in short supply.

A good many British traditions endure, especially in Parliament and the provincial legislatures — one of which, in Quebec, is known as the National Assembly, a bit of swank that nobody seems to mind any more. Nobody minds the premier of Quebec being called prime minister, because in French "premier" means "prime" and is only half a title. The rest of the premiers achieve equal treatment by being called "first minister," and nobody suggests they shorten it to "first."

Often the customs brought from Britain are preserved in more archaic fashion than in the Mother of Parliaments. Witness the story from Saskatchewan when there was disorder in the legislature and the Speaker wanted to name an offending member in order to eject him but couldn't recall the member's name. So he signalled to the sergeant-at-arms, shouting: "To arms, Sergeant!" That gentleman, new to his post, leaped to his feet and tried to draw his sword from its scabbard. But the weapon had been encased there for years and was rusted in, so the legislature was treated to the sight of the bedecked and beribboned sergeant-at-arms lurching up and down the aisle, plucking at his sword to no avail. The session wound up in total disorder.

Another Speaker, George Black of the federal House of Commons, lived in his chambers in the Centre Block of Parliament Hill and kept a gun beside his chosen armchair. His favourite sport was to pot rabbits and squirrels through the open window, causing the sound of gunfire to echo through the corridors and across the lawns of Parliament. Anybody who suggested he stop was told, in the fashion of Speaker Black's native Yukon, to go to hell.

The Hill has always been a place for good hunting because, in addition to the resident groundhogs, rabbits, and squirrels, the precincts are visited by wandering bears, moose, deer, and various specimens of our national animal, the beaver. The largest beaver ever found in the neighbourhood weighed forty-five pounds and was removed from one of the Rideau Canal locks at the base of Parliament Hill, where it was busy building a dam. Usually, visiting beaver are crated and returned to the wilderness, which begins just across the river from Ottawa and stretches all the way to the North Pole. But this one was skinned, cooked, and eaten, and those present at the feast pronounced it delicious, with the colour and texture of Canada Goose. We are the only country in the world with both a national animal and a national bird that are edible. Do the British eat lions, or have you ever seen an American or a German eat an eagle? Russians eat bears, and so do we, but they don't taste as good as beaver.

What Canada is chiefly noted for in the rest of the world is cold weather, and the inhabitants spend much of their time fighting it and fleeing to warmer climes where their dollar is worth only half as much as it is at home. Despite this tendency, nobody cheered at the prospect of having a Caribbean province, when the Turks and Caicos islands wanted in. The late Max Saltsman, when he was a New Democrat MP, fought for the deal but got nowhere, though it had everything going for it.

This was the second time Canada missed the tropical boat, the first being when the king of Hawaii wrote to Sir John A. Macdonald asking if Canada would be interested in having Hawaii as a province, to save it from the clutches of Uncle Sam. Sir John asked an aide if there was anything worth having in Hawaii, and he was told it was nothing but sun and sand. Neither of those items was held in high regard in those days, when mountains were in fashion. Nobody told Sir John that Hawaii had some splendid mountains, so he threw the letter away without answering it and we lost our chance.

The world loves Canada for the Calgary Stampede, where broncos buck because they have a belt cinched around their vitals (take a close look next time — you'd buck too!). And the world hates Canada for the seal hunt, which provided a living for hard-up fishermen. So the seal hunt has been stamped out, along with the Star Kist tuna plant, which was the only means of livelihood in the impoverished southeast corner of New Brunswick. Nobody died of tainted tuna, nobody even got sick from it, but it almost overthrew the government, which gives an idea of how happy a place Canada is.

Canada is known to Americans chiefly for bacon, whisky, and smoked salmon, known to the Jewish clientele south of the border as Nova Scotia lox, or just plain "nova." Our disasters get equal treatment in the U.S. press with the horrors that happen elsewhere, and there is a running commentary there about the weather we send them, which on the whole is less well received than our Christmas trees, Wayne Gretzky, Margaret Atwood, or even Farley Mowat. Marshall McLuhan was popular with Americans who pretended to understand him, which no Canadian did, though God knows we tried.

Nobody says much about the way English is spoken in Canada. Apart from the lilt of Newfoundland, the gutterals of Lunenburg, and the dialect of the Ottawa Valley, there is a single accent across the country. Pierre Trudeau always maintained that most Quebeckers speak lousy French, a suspicion confirmed by most Frenchmen who visit our shores. One Quebec political leader, Réal Caouette of the Créditistes, boasted that his wartime heroes were Hitler and Mussolini, but he diverted the uproar in the rest of the country by saying France was a backward land where even the toilets didn't work. Anglos cheered.

People live for a long time in Prince Edward Island, which is to Canada what the Caucasus region is to the Soviet Union in terms of the longevity of its residents. There was a premier, Walter Shaw, who was seventy-five when he was in office, and he lived a long time after that. He asked a neighbouring farmer, also in his mid-seventies, if he was going to finish the ploughing that day, and this exchange took place:

"Could, but I ain't."

"Why not, John?"

"Gotta go to a weddin'."

"Who's getting married?"

"Me father."

"Glory, John, how old is he?"

"He be ninety-four."

"No, why would a man ninety-four want to get married?"

"Doesn't wanta. Hasta!"

Most Canadian jokes these days are about Newfoundlanders, the best of them told by Newfs themselves. Here are three told by Don Jamieson when he was fat and sassy in the Trudeau cabinet:

A Newfoundland couple stayed late at their own wedding reception and headed down the road after midnight with no fixed destination, stopping at the first place that had a sign "room to rent." An elderly man answered the door and asked if they were married, and the groom indicated the confetti in his hair. The man asked them to step into the parlour and demanded the marriage licence. The groom offered his driver's licence, and the man said he wasn't sure, "but yez kin go upstairs and I'll check with me daughter when she gets in shortly."

When the daughter arrived the man told about the couple upstairs and showed the licence, whereupon the daughter gasped: "Daddy, Daddy! This is not a marriage licence! This is a driver's licence!"

"Holy Jesus!" exclaimed the man, and he rushed up the stairs two at a time, pounding on the bedroom door and shouting: "Bye! Bye! If yez hasn't done her yet, don't do her, 'cause dis ain't fer dat!"

And then there was the aviator stunting in an open-cockpit plane without a parachute, and he fell out. Tumbling earthward, he uttered a prayer to St. Francis and suddenly a great hand reached out from a cloud and arrested his fall.

"Oh, St. Francis! St. Francis! Bless you!" cried the hapless chap.

A voice thundered: "You calling Xavier, or Assisi?"

The man thought for a second, and blurted "Xavier," thinking of Brian Mulroney's alma mater.

"Sorry," said the voice, and the hand flipped.

And consider the Newfoundlander who went to Toronto and showed up at a fancy house of ill perfume, inquiring if there was a girl there named Carol. The madame said there was, but that she was the top girl and there were others just as nice a lot cheaper. The lad insisted on Carol and the madame said very well, but he would be wasting his money. He went up and met Carol, and gladly paid his $200 at the end of the encounter.

Next night he returned, said he wanted Carol again, and shook off the madame's low-cost alternatives. Another great encounter, and another 200 bucks.

Third night, the same thing, and when it was over he really had Carol's attention and she asked him where he was from. He said Corner Brook, and she smiled and said she thought as much, because she was from there herself.

"What street?" she asked.

"Humber."

"What a coincidence!" said Carol. "Me too. What number?"

"350."

"This is amazing," said Carol. "I grew up next door at 352."

"I know," smiled the young man. "Your mother gave me $600 to bring for you!"

And Jamieson tells the story about politicians arriving at the pearly gates and being told by St. Peter that the only way to heaven was up a ladder, on each rung of which they had to write, in chalk, a promise they had not kept. Brian Mulroney took chalk in hand and started his ascent, but halfway up the ladder somebody stepped on his fingers. It was Pierre Trudeau, coming down for more chalk!

It used to be the fashion in the House of Commons for MPs to make setpiece speeches on subjects close to their hearts, and these became trademarks. One such was Lloyd Crouse from Lunenburg, Nova Scotia, one of the last of the true free enterprisers in politics. For years it was Crouse's custom to uncork his speech on the glories of private enterprise, as practised by himself as an entrepreneur in his home town. More of Crouse in a moment — suffice it to say he grew weary of trying to persuade his Commons colleagues of the merits of the marketplace and stopped making the speech, especially after he was passed over by two Tory prime ministers, Joe Clark and Brian Mulroney, as being too hot to handle for a cabinet post.

Another annual speech that caused horror in the chamber came from John Blackmore, the Social Credit member for Lethbridge and a precursor of James Keegstra who fouled Alberta's name in the 1980s. Blackmore held the seat for wentythree years, from 1935 until John Diefenbaker brought him down in 1958. During the 1930s it was Blackmore's custom to make an annual speech in the Commons about the perils of the Jewish conspiracy to take over the world. Nobody paid much attention, but after Canada's entry into the war against Nazi Germany it was suggested to Blackmore that he might usefully put his speech to rest, at least until the war was over. Blackmore needed some persuading, but finally settled for retaining the bulk of the speech, changing only one reference. Wherever the word "Jewish" occurred he substituted "Turco-Mongolian." And that's the way you'll find it in Hansard, until Blackmore wearied of the message.

Back to Crouse. He operated a trawler that came under a new law governing the size of net that could be used to catch various species of fish. When his vessel came into port he asked the captain if it had been a successful voyage. "Yes," said the captain, "and no." When Crouse asked why, the captain said: "Well, Lloyd, under that new law you passed, we have to decide before going out what kind of fish we're after, big or small. And that means we have to take either the big mesh net for the big fish, or the little mesh net for the small fish. So I elects for the little mesh net and we gets out there and there are no small fish, so the voyage shapes up as a failure. But then I thinks, well, you can't catch the little fish in the big mesh net but you can catch the big fish in the little mesh net, so I sets her out where the big fish is and we fills the boat.

"But on our way in I gets to thinkin', by golly, there's Lloyd up in Parliament and he passed that law and he's the owner of this wessel and he'll be in terrible trouble if we gets caught. So I gives instructions to cut away the gear and throw it all overboard, which we did."

"Golly, captain," gasped Crouse. "How much was the gear worth?"

"Well," says the captain, "I estimate about $10,000. And when I see it going over the side I thinks that you passed a very stupid law, eh? But I suppose you knows what you're doing."

Another Lunenburg story has to do with a Captain Publicover, age ninety-two, being interviewed by Frank Willis of the CBC, who asks if it's true the captain was a great man for the ladies.

"Yes, lad," says the captain, "never went on a voyage without one, if I could help it."

"When was your last voyage?"

"Last year, took a schooner into New York."

"Did you take a girlie with you?"

"Deed I did," grinned the captain. "And a nice one, too. At my age, it takes a little longer, but I don't begrudge the time!"

One last Newfoundland story, about a fisherman being interviewed by Don MacNeil, then of CBC, about the offshore oil discoveries.

"Dey's going to booger it up," says the fisherman.

"Who is?"

"The mainlanders. Dey boogers everyting oop when dey comes here."

"How will they bugger up the offshore oil?"

"I'll tell you, bye, dey's going to drill ten feet too deep out there and the whole damn ocean going to drain out thru the hole!"

And a final Crouse yarn. A Lunenburg captain took his son out in their little Tancook schooner for a day's sail and they got caught in a storm and had to anchor overnight in a sheltered island cove. The wind blew all night, and in the morning there was fog. The boy went on deck and found there was no sign of land, the anchor rope having come apart.

"Fadder! Fadder!" he cried. "We ain't heah!"

The father rushed up on deck and said: "Begads you're right, son, we ain't widdin ten miles of heah!" He looked astern and shouted: "Trow out the spare anchor!"

"But fadder," protested the lad, "there's no rope on her."

"Trow her out anyways," said the father. "She'll help a little!"

My favourite Parliáment Hill joke was about the tourist who heard the division bells ringing and asked the Hon. Waldo Monteith what they meant. Monty, not usually a man of quick wit, shot back: "I think one of them must have escaped!"

A true one involved Walter Dinsdale, a devout Salvationist who was Northern Affairs minister in John Diefenbaker's cabinet and approved the expenditure of $3 million to restore Arizona Charlie's Palace Grand Saloon in Dawson City as a tourist attraction. Having inspected the rebuilt premises, and noting that there were bedrooms behind the mezzanine stalls in the theatre, I told Walter it seemed he had spent a lot of money to restore a whorehouse.

"Never!" said the minister.

"Well, what about those bedrooms?"

"You see, the place was used as a Sunday school during the Gold Rush, and the bedrooms were so the children could take their naps!"

There's been a lot of talk about grace under pressure, and nobody shows more of it than Her Majesty the Queen during her sojourns in our midst. On one occasion, during the great royal tour of 1959 when she was pregnant with Prince Andrew, she was taken to an Indian settlement on Vancouver Island and inspected a row of teepees along the beach. A terrible smell hung over the encampment, and as the royal party progressed the smell got stronger and stronger. Finally, in front of the last teepee, the Queen approached a huge iron cauldron that was boiling over an open fire and exuding the effluvium that had other members of the party reeling. Her Majesty stuck her head over the rim of the pot and the Indian woman who was in charge stuck a paddle into the mess and gave it a stir, agitating the fish guts, fish heads, bones and other ingredients and creating a huge cloud of steam that engulfed the Queen. When the air cleared the Queen came back into view, not even blinking, much less throwing up. She smiled, and said in her sweetest voice, without a quiver, "How nice!"

My favourite story about Philip on royal tours was the one he told himself in a speech to the Ottawa Canadian Club, when he noted that in pidgin English he was known as "fella belong Mrs. Queen."

That same audience heard Roland Michener, when he was Governor General, tell a story about President Charles de Gaulle of France. De Gaulle was on a tour of South America and was headed for Uruguay when he discovered nobody aboard the plane knew the name of the Uruguayan president, an office that used to change hands yearly. An urgent message was dispatched from the plane to the French foreign minister, Giscard d'Estaing, in Paris.

"Do you know who is the president of Uruguay?" de Gaulle queried.

Back came the reply: "Oui."

"Bien," was the further query, "mais oui, qui?"

And the answer: "Oui, mon général!"

Many an adventure story has come out of the North (Canada is so big in three directions that we always capitalize North, East, and West. But we are so shallow to the south that we never capitalize that, there being no such place, unless of course you happen to live in the North, in which case the south is known as "outside.") It was in the North that the mighty Hodgson held sway, for a dozen weird and mostly wonderful years.

Our Once and Only Emperor

Stuart Hodgson was the first resident commissioner of the Northwest Territories and the only Canadian administrator ever to comport himself as an emperor, apart of course from the mandarins in Ottawa. Hodgson really was an emperor, and he got away with it and kept telling the Ottawa bosses to go to hell. Many of us looked forward to the royal commission when Hodgson would be deposed, but he outsmarted everyone and it never happened.

At one point during his reign the minister for northern affairs, Jean Chrétien, phoned Hodgson and told him the Liberals wanted him to run for the Territories seat in the next federal election.

"Nothing doing," said Hodgson, "I like it here."

"If you don't run, we're going to fire you," said Chrétien.

Long pause on the radio telephone.

"Repeat that," Hodgson asked. Chrétien did.

"Now, Mr. Minister," said Hodgson, "I just want to say one thing, and I'm only going to say it once. If you retract that threat, I'll promise not to run up here for the opposition!"

There was spluttering at the Ottawa end, as there always was when Hodgson was going his own way, but nothing more was heard.

It was my privilege to travel vast distances in the North in Hodgson's company, and to see the regard with which he was held by the Inuit and Indian people, however much the intellectuals may have scorned him. Wherever he went he had us building cairns, some with survival kits in them, and we lugged more rocks and built more cairns than there are on Easter Island. He made us dig huge holes to bury empty oil drums, in a vain effort to clean up the North. Some of Hodgson's cairns were twelve feet high, visible for long distances across the tundra, and the best that could be said for them was that he did most of the work himself, while the rest of us lagged.

Following his twelve years as emperor of the North, Hodgson was appointed co-chairman of the International Joint Commission. When he came back from his first visit to Washington he was in a state of great excitement. "Washington," he reported, "is no hell, but Geez, have they ever got a wonderful cairn there! God, how I'd love to have THAT in the North!" Turned out he was talking about the Washington Monument.

As emperor of the North, Hodgson aroused feelings of either awe or outrage. His one-time colleagues in the New Democratic Party tried repeatedly to get him canned, though he was the only union man to rise to the heights of political power and the only ruler to speak in double negatives and make them sound right. I think it had something to do with his height and the way he towered over people, especially our northern natives, who tend to be built close to the ice so they don't lose their balance.

I was with Hodgson on a memorable day when he dropped his borrowed Twin Otter aircraft down beside the Arctic Sound encampment of Simon Kadlum, a carver noted for his soapstone chessboards. Simon and his family were summering in their favourite spot, and his teenage daughter was mincing about on the beach in high-heeled shoes and store-bought clothes, as pretty as any southern city belle. He showed us a chessboard he was working on with his worn old jackknife, and it was beautiful, though only half finished. Simon said he couldn't finish it because he had run out of the stone for the white squares, and would have to wait until winter when he could go across the ice to the island where his soapstone quarry was located. He figured the ice would be firm by December, and then it would be a ten-day trip out by dogsled and ten days back, with a few days for the digging. Then he could get back to his chessboards.

Hodgson got that look on his face that comes over him in moments of inspiration — a brightening of the eyes, a quivering of the lips, a wiggling of the ears and a waving of the arms, and a conspiratorial chuckle, followed by a pronouncement. In such moments, Hodgson was not given to proposing — he pronounced. And what he pronounced on this occasion was that if Simon would get his digging gear ready by 9 o'clock the next morning we would drop in on him again with our faithful aircraft, pick him up, fly him to his island, help him dig out enough soapstone to keep him going for the balance of the summer — and buy two chessboards from him.

It was an offer he couldn't refuse. When we flew in on him at the appointed hour the next morning from our base in Bathurst Inlet, Simon was waiting on the shore with his pack, shovel, and three canvas bags for the rock. Away we went, with Simon's wondering womenfolk waving us off. No sooner were we aloft than we encountered that phenomenon of the North — the fact that Inuit, who never lose their way on land, sea, or ice, became disoriented when aloft, and Simon couldn't figure which way we were to go to reach his island. The pilot pulled out a map and, after long contemplation, Simon put his finger on a speck and said he thought that might be it. We turned in that direction and in an hour we were there. We circled a couple of times so Simon could get his bearings, and finally he nodded and indicated where we should land. The pilot made a rough-seas landing and got us to the shore, where we unloaded our gear and agreed to a pick-up two hours hence.

Simon pointed to a mountain that was the island's dominant feature, indicating with his finger that the soapstone deposit was about half way up. I groaned, but Hodgson grabbed the pick and shovel, slung them over his shoulder, and said: "Let's go."

Go we did, straight up as it seemed to me, and after what felt like hours of climbing we reached the magic spot and Simon started to pound away with his pick. But each chunk of stone he dug out he examined and discarded — continuing this procedure until, almost an hour after he had started, he still didn't have any keepers. We indicated with some urgency that the plane would be returning soon, and that he had better start saving some rock, so he gave a mighty blow and the whole mountainside started to shift.

Hodgson was standing directly below the place where Simon was excavating, and it was clear that if there were a rockslide, the emperor of the North was going to become the first ruler ever to be buried in a mound of soapstone. Simon leaped to one side but Hodgson stood his ground, because there was no place for him to go. He just stood there, staring, while the earth moved, and then slowly everything came to rest.

"Stu!" I shouted, half relieved, half admiring his calm in the face of near disaster. "If you had been buried you're lucky we have the carver right here. What would you have liked over you — a polar bear, or a walrus?"

"Bastard," he snorted. "Tell Simon to get some rock out, pronto!"

The big slide had loosened some good stones, so Simon filled two bags and Hodgson and I headed down to the shore, shouldering loads that must have weighed fifty kilos, or so they felt. Hodgson made the trip half on the run and I panted along behind. When we dumped the stone we carried the empty bags back up, where Simon had another pile waiting, so we loaded up again, and down we went. We made three trips before the plane returned, and when we got back aboard we must have had 300 kilos of prime soapstone, both light and dark varieties, chessboards in the raw.

We delivered Simon back, in triumph, to his Arctic Sound encampment and unloaded the stone. He promised to set to work, and we paid him in advance for two chessboards with the pieces to go with them — seals for the pawns, igloos for the castles, walruses for the bishops, Simon and his wife for the king and queen, bears for the knights.

Months later my chessboard arrived, a thing of beauty that remains a prized possession, the more so because I carried that stone myself. But my son Daniel, the anthropologist, deflated me with a denunciation to the effect that we had probably spoiled Simon for life, leaving him to stand on a beach waiting for an airplane, instead of planning his mining expedition according to the ice conditions. "You have made him," said son, "a dependant — a ward of our society."

Awash in a gulf of guilt, I made subsequent inquiries and determined that Simon was prospering. Far from losing his initiative, he was making annual treks to the mine, and his chessboards were getting better and better, which is saying something.

Simon has fared better than Inuit trapper William Koaha, now gone to his reward on the great trapline in the sky, but in his prime one of the great dancers and drummers of Bathurst Inlet. William was away, feeding his dogs on a remote island, when word came that Governor General Ed Schreyer was going to visit Bathurst Inlet Lodge with his entourage. Hodgson, having relinquished his empire the year before, was making a return visit to his former domains and took charge of arrangements to greet the Commander-in-Chief at the lodge, including a summons to William to come in from the bush and do his stuff for His Ex.

The night before the Schreyers were to arrive, William came in and a warm-up party was arranged, in the course of which the nomads of Bathurst Inlet entertained us and, egged on by Hodgson and the grape, we entertained back. A fine time was had by all, and William danced and drummed himself into a stupor. Finally, we all said goodnight beneath the midnight sun and went to bed, with packs of wolves howling us to our rest.

Next morning the Schreyers arrived, and the vice-regal pennant was hoisted on the lodge flagstaff. Vast preparations were made for the feast and celebration that night, with special commands from Hodgson about the songs I was to sing, including our Press Gallery version of "Lily the Pink," in honour of Her Excellency. I worked over the words, to the tune of the Lydia Pinkham Vegetable Compound song:

Oh, we drink a drink a drink
To Lily the Pink a Pink a Pink
The Chatelaine of Rideau Ha-ha-hall!
We'll never tire, of Lily Schreyer,
To us Her Ex is Ten Feet Tall!

Schreyer was taken on an aerial exploration of Wilberforce Falls, and insisted on landing on a lake and visiting the falls by foot. This resulted in a late return to the lodge, by which time we had determined that William, the star of the evening's vice-regal entertainment, was nowhere to be found. Word was he had returned to the island where his dogs were.

As soon as the plane got back it was dispatched to fetch him, guided by his wife who, as usual, lost her bearings once the plane was in the air. But by diligent circling, and aided by the fact that the sun never sets on Hodgson's empire in summer, the place was found and William was rooted out of his lean-to.

Why had he defected? Did he not know that the Governor General was expecting him?

Governor? General?

William was bewildered. He knew about the Queen. And he knew about Hodgson. As far as he was concerned, when he had performed in Hodgson's presence, that was it. There was nobody else who mattered.

No, we said, Schreyer was higher.

This was news to William, but he agreed to board the aircraft as long as we'd get him back next morning. So we got him to the lodge, and he performed, and we performed, and a good time was had by all. But to the day of his death, William never did understand who that other guy was. Hodgson, as far as he was concerned, was emperor.

And for all the self-government that has prevailed in the Territories since, I suspect a lot of natives still imagine that the seat of all real power was Emperor Hodgson.

Love in the Third Solitude

Keith Spicer, when he was Canada's first commissioner for official languages, advocated that English-speaking Ottawa men hie themselves across the river to Hull and consort with the women of Quebec, who would have them speaking French in jig time. There is no evidence that Spicer's advice bore fruit, and he himself went to British Columbia for a refresher course in Anglo isolation, returning to Ottawa as editor of what must be the most profitable English-language daily newspaper in the country.

As one who took Spicer's suggested language course to heart, I can tell him he left out one simple factor. If an English-speaking man is to learn our other maternal language by consorting with a French-speaking woman, it is important that she know no English. In my happy case, the object of my affections, coming as she did from Montreal, had made herself fluent in English, and as a result knew my own language better than I knew it myself. She knew all the songs, all the jokes, all the cuss words, and even all the accents, imitating the Queen and a Lunenburg fisherman with equal fluency.

Claudy Mailly had been a policy adviser to John Crosbie during the 1979 regime of Joe Clark, and she helped Crosbie put together the "boodjit" on which that government fell. Crosbie used to call her his "frankyphone" and warned her, on visits to Newfoundland, to keep her trap shut "because down here we keep you people in enclaves." Their good-humoured relationship may have deluded Crosbie into thinking he could jolly Quebeckers into supporting his later leadership bid, when he likened his lack of French to his inability to speak Chinese. Claudy still has the secret papers on which that ill-fated 1979 budget was based, buried deep in our basement under a stack of cardboard boxes containing the hoarded refuse of my fifty years in journalism and her twenty-five years in assorted toil, including bookkeeper to the Seafarers' International Union health plan when the union was run by Hal Banks. She wrote a fine novel that caused a stir in Quebec literary and political circles, in the thick of the Quiet Revolution. She was wife to a Montreal advertising executive from the Anglo side of the Two Solitudes, mother of what appears to be a genius son, owner of her own PR firm, world traveller à la early Trudeau, adviser to giant corporations and bank presidents, and candidate for Parliament, first a big loser, then a bigger winner.

Her mother named all her children after movie stars, and Claudy was from Claudette Colbert. The two of us encountered Miss Colbert with Rex Harrison in 1984, during a visit to the Cotswolds, and the grand old actress seemed unimpressed when I told her my love was named after her. She sniffed that she wasn't sure about the Claudy bit, so we broke off the exchange and Colbert went her way, and we went ours, the last we heard being Rex Harrison's chuckle.

We met on Joe Clark's campaign plane in the final two weeks of the election that cost Clark his prime ministership. When I saw her, in the Tory press room in Moncton, I asked who the hell was that and was told it was Mme. Mailly, in charge of herding the French press gang on the tour, and Joe Clark's coach for his interviews and speeches in French. On our way to Clark's meeting in Moncton she asked to borrow my newspaper, and life has never been the same since for either of us.

The next day in Summerside she was in charge of press arrangements for Clark's speech to the Chamber of Commerce, which involved making sure that we didn't get any of the luncheon food. The Chamber was uneasy about hearing a politician during an election campaign, and did not want any publicity. We could smell the food from the room in which we were incarcerated, and Mme. Mailly said she thought it was turnips. I said carrots, so we checked, and turnips it was. Mashed turnips.

When I challenged her to dinner that night we went to Charlottetown's one swanky restaurant and she said she craved turnip, but the maitre d' said there wasn't a turnip in the place. I asked that he send out into the town in quest of a turnip and he was impressed enough to do so, while we sat in the bar drinking Chivas Regal, as was madame's habit when media people were spending their boss's money on her. After four slugs of Chivas had been disposed of, the maitre d' returned in triumph to report that a turnip had been located, and how would Madame like it done? Sliced, and sautéed in butter, said she. And so, in due course, we sat down to this beautifully prepared turnip, and I don't remember what else, and she told me later that any man who would put forward such effort to satisfy a companion's desires, including a craving for turnip, could not be all bad.

For six years we have proceeded roughly on that pattern, and my French has improved hardly at all, between bouts of laughter during the happy times and tears when it gets stormy. We have embraced in English and fought in English. When she throws me out, bag and baggage, the epithets are in English, as are the reconciliations, most of which are warm enough to make up for the icy ousters, some of which have seen me tramp the vacant streets of Ottawa all night, with no place to lay my head. God damn you, Spicer, I have muttered through many a dawn, you didn't say anything about this. And I have blessed Spicer within hours of uttering that curse.

When the wife of one of the French senators chided me for not improving my French under Claudy's tutelage, I said we always spoke English because she didn't want me to miss anything important.

"Get her to speak French to you after midnight," said Mme. Senator.

"But that is when many important things are said," I replied.

To which my adviser retorted: "Get her to translate it for you in the morning."

We have tried French-speaking days, speak-French-on-the-phone days, read-French days, and attendance at functions where nothing but French is spoken, my chief breakthrough being to know when to laugh even though I don't get the joke.

My favourite word is "d'accord," which encourages French-speakers to keep on talking, though it can get you into trouble if they want you to expand. My most dreaded word is "alors," uttered by the loved one after a long conversation with a friend or colleague on the telephone. There are no short phone conversations in French, but inevitably they start to peter out after half an hour or so and you get the feeling they are about to terminate so you can get back to the meal, or the drink, or whatever, when suddenly Madame utters the awful "alors," and they are off on another topic. I have known conversations with as many as five "alors" in them, especially dismaying because I have never had a true translation of the word and do not believe one exists. The best I can do is "so," or "well then," which can lead to a summing up of the topic just discussed, or a turning to another subject entirely.

Needless to say, I have yet to resort to use of the word "alors" myself. I am too busy dealing with Claudy's views on the media business and its outpourings, which she punctuates with well-placed expletives in English, such as bullshit and asshole.

The complications in our lives have been many, all of them worthwhile given the compensations. Since we joined company she has continued her eventful professional life, giving me an inside look at a practising feminist in action, mostly in French, thus enabling me to bridge four solitudes in what some critics have called my terminal delirium.

She blew away my claims to be a pioneer feminist, and in vain have I shown her my 1961 article in *Chatelaine*, advocating an end to women's clubs and auxiliaries and full acceptance of women into what was then a man's world. I spoke of the natural intellectual superiority of Canadian women over Canadian men, saying that with every couple I had known the woman was the mental superior of the man, and conversation with women much more stimulating than with men. "You just wanted to lay them," she pronounced, and that was the end of that, as though she had decided what new shade of wallpaper she wanted for the hall.

In vain did I protest my early and prolonged enlightenment.

She would have none of it, though she rejected my credentials more in pity than in anger, admitting that as men went there was hope, even though I said some of the right things for all the wrong reasons. Occasionally I would blow my top and say that smart people caused more trouble in the world than stupid ones, and that would be a three-day job to patch up, neither of us ever apologizing for things said, however horrible.

I still haven't figured her sensitivity to praise of other women, and I can't believe she really thinks I'm always horny, though some think most men are perpetually in that condition, and others never. It can lead to some interesting exchanges, most inconclusive, and some very happily concluded indeed. She says it would be a big help if I would stop panting when other women heave into view, and just treat them like people. God knows I try, and protest that my panting has nothing to do with jiggling bazooms or wiggling buttocks or quivering nostrils when a stranger of the female sex approaches and says, "You don't remember me, do you?" My response, "What unforgettable experience did we share?" usually backs them off, but by then Claudy is out the door, revolted. In her best moments Claudy calls our life "Paradiso," raising her voice in song. In her worst times she says the whole trip has been a bummer, and says the Irish are worse than the Scots, her first husband having been a Scot.

This is one of her more accurate appraisals and I have seen her make many, starting with the Clark re-election campaign in 1980 which she knew in advance he had lost, though she didn't share this view with those of us in media. In fact, she has never shared any of her party secrets with me, which has handicapped me in my work while enriching my life. In the final days of that campaign she radiated confidence that her man Joe would win, and I remember her urging my colleague, Ben Tierney, to pray for a Trudeau defeat. Ben, sitting at the bar of the Sheraton Brock in Niagara Falls, cast his eyes upward and prayed.

"Ben," I said, "how long since you've prayed?"

"Not since I was a wee bairn in Glasgy," came the reply.

"Then your prayers will do Clark no good," I said. "Nobody up there will be listening."

"Och, no," said Ben, "what they'll say is Jesus, if Tierney's praying, this must be important!"

Ben's prayers weren't answered, and out went the Tories, and Claudy wound up in the party's research office in Ottawa, a hotbed of intrigue and backstabbing as is the Tory custom whether the party is in or out of office. She fought for her place and encountered numerous frustrations while the party tried to make up its mind about Clark's leadership. Many people sought her advice about Quebec, and nobody took it, and finally Clark demanded a loyalty oath from all party workers and they wound up firing her. She sued the party and collected.

Dissident Tory MPs found a place for her on The Hill, in the office of MP Elmer MacKay, the main plotting centre for the movement to oust Clark in favour of Brian Mulroney. Mulroney's work had caught Claudy's eye, and vice versa. She eked out her meagre parliamentary pay by writing speeches for Quebec Tory senators, and when Mulroney started spouting she wrote drafts for him, too. Living with all of this was like being on a roller coaster, not a bad place to be if you're past sixty and starting to grieve for departed friends and dread your own decline into the final vale of tears. We travelled together, fished together, wined and dined and spread joy, and Mulroney won the leadership. The woman who became his press secretary was Claudy, at peril of her life, her limbs, and her sanity, though she came to the job with few illusions about media and left it with none.

She had run as a Tory candidate in the 1979 election won by Joe Clark. Her opponent in the Montreal riding of Papineau was the Hon. André Ouellet, and she got clobbered. Her ambition was to run again, and so it was that after months coping with the media hordes around Mulroney (in the course of which the press was good to him but rough on her, indicating she must have been doing something right), he told her to get ready to run. The designated riding was Gatineau, across the river from Ottawa.

And that was almost the last I saw of her for several months leading to the election call by the newly installed prime minister, John Turner, in office so briefly that he made Joe Clark look durable. She injected herself into the life of Gatineau so thoroughly you would think she had lived there all her life, quite an achievement for a kid from East End Montreal with all the street smarts, scars, hangups, and skills acquired in that notorious hotbed of passion, violence, crime, and survival. She had wielded a paddle in the jam factory at age twelve, and from age five, she claims, had fled from the roving hands of horny curés and the blows of flinty-eyed nuns. She had cried only when, on successive pilgrimages to Quebec City as she carried candles in the street processions, the wind blew her candle flame against the side of the paper shield and the whole thing went up in flames. What she says she said, through her tears, was "shit!" or "Merde — pas encore!"

And so it was that on election night 1984, everybody but herself having predicted her defeat, she took to her hotel-room tub with a glass of cognac, satisfied she had done her best and happy that Mulroney had brought his big campaign jet into Gatineau Airport on the final Friday night, the biggest thing in town since Champlain passed through the territory 370 years before. Three minutes after the polls closed, son Ian knocked on the bathroom door and hailed "my mother, the MP." The media computers declared her elected before anybody else. There was a big victory celebration in the local spaghetti house which I missed because I was in Toronto covering the election on radio, a hard place to get tidings from the Gatineau.

Since then, life with the Hon. Member has taught me a little French and more about The French than most Anglos ever know. And more about politics than media people dream of, relating especially to the casework of the constituency. I have eaten corn and lobsters and danced the nights away, got lost on dirt roads, and sat up late waiting for her to come home by jeep and snowmobile. I have revelled in her smiles at a meeting gone well, and reflected her scowls at "those bastards," be they political enemies or media critics. And I have seen her roll her eyes upward at my own writings, usually with the words: "Surely, you knew..." How was I to know when she wouldn't tell me anything, and nobody else in the party would either, assuming she had?

We have a pact not to discuss her politics or my writings, so we won't exert undue influence on one another and thus risk warping one another's work. The pact is violated daily, but we've only come to blows once, and I got the worst of it both physically and psychologically, though the making up was a wondrous thing.

I have become the best-informed squarehead reporter in the country, in terms of understanding Quebec and the people who live there, and the House of Commons and the people who work there. And the riding of Gatineau I know like the back of my true love's hand, sharing her dreams and telling her that the great buildings we have seen in Europe really would look out of place in the riding, and that the bridge she wants across the river doesn't really need to be as beautiful as the Pont Alexandre III in Paris, with all its cherubs and curlicues.

"The riding has the biggest woodpile in the world," I say, pointing to the mountain of logs by the CIP mill. "What more do you want?"

"Jobs," says she. "Jobs, jobs, jobs." Mulroney used that line first, in the 1984 election, and I suspect she wrote it for him.

Thirty years of writing newspaper columns resulted in a brusqueness of speech that sounds offensive to French speakers, who favour elaboration, especially on emotional themes. Early in our relationship, Madame collided with my usual method of expressing dissent, which is to say "Wrong!" After enduring this response for as long as she could, she suggested perhaps I could stop saying that and instead try to engage the subject under discussion, outlining my position in opposition to hers, with as much documentation and supporting evidence as I could muster.

Thus did I try to enter into the minefield of sane and sober debate, but my years of journalism finally did me in, and after she had expressed herself on a certain topic, while we were walking on a downtown street, I retorted with the opinion that she had just uttered the biggest piece of horseshit I had ever heard in my life. She stopped walking, turned, and regarded me in silence. And then she said: "I think perhaps we had better go back to 'wrong.'"

I've tried to do better, but my newspaper training continues to get in the way — what Claudy calls the natural arrogance of the breed. Indeed, it's hard to be humble. Milady insists that we in the newspaper business have much to be modest about, though modesty is not much in fashion in the trade. It is a thought that has occurred to me from time to time, and I have even given voice to it, though not daring to put it into practice for fear of being trampled by confreres seeking their turn at the turf.

I was thirty-seven years old, and more than twenty years into my newspaper career, when I made my first public speech to an audience, in Hamilton, Ontario. I was United Nations correspondent for the CBC at the time, and fresh from covering Mike Pearson winning, as it turned out, Canada's first and only Nobel Peace Prize. I discovered two things on that occasion — that I enjoyed talking to live audiences more than I did talking to TV cameras or microphones, and that press reports on a speech seldom bear much resemblance to what the speaker said.

At least a thousand speeches later, I am still looking for what I regard as an accurate report on any speech of mine, and count it a net gain if, as usually happens, the local press ignores the visiting speaker entirely. I speak without notes, a practice that audiences appreciate but which is interpreted by media people as a hostile act — print people hate it because they have to stay for the speech, and TV people say they can't shoot the event if they don't know in advance where the good parts are. Tell them they're all good parts, and they fall down laughing. Tell them you don't know what you're going to say until you're on your feet, and they turn away in disgust. Tell them it's mostly jokes, funny stories, songs and dances, and they pack up. But whatever they do, they never tell it the way you think it is. Often, they report it the way they think you would have said it, if you knew what you were talking about. Sometimes it's the opposite of what you said, or intended to say. Invariably, paraphrases appear inside quotation marks. Politicians have known this always, and the Hon. Member has lived with it all her life.

Nothing will stop this, and there is no way the full flavour of a speech can be conveyed in print or clips. Fair enough, but it is important to remember that a prime minister making a policy speech is subjected to the same treatment as the strolling player at the local Canadian Club — except that in the case of the prime minister, the reporters tend to be pundits-in-waiting, imparting their slant to the speech, usually snide.

Years of mistreatment at the hands of the newest reporter on the staff have led me to think that every reporter should make at least one public speech and endure the hazards of being reported upon — not in journalism class or closed seminar, but right out there in public. That would give a clear idea of what public figures and politicians endure at our hands, and it might even encourage us to do better and not insist that audiences forevermore must endure the reading of written texts because media will punish those who speak off the cuff.

Remember that speeches, like writings, are worth what people will pay for them, so there could be money to be made at the podium. Some of us have been known to make more in half an hour on our feet than we make in a week at the keyboard or on the tube. And look how humble it keeps us!

Our Wonderful One-Hoss Sleighs

If a thing is Canadian, Canadians assume there must be something wrong with it. They treat it with suspicion, the way they respond to "How are you?" with the cautious "Not too bad" or "Could be worse" or "Surviving."

The great Canadian inventions of the twentieth century have been the variable-pitch propeller and the snowmobile. We responded to the variable-pitch propeller by ignoring it — I only know about it because it was invented by a neighbour of my family by the name of Turnbull, in Saint John, New Brunswick, and I learned to dance in the arms of his grand-daughter, Arras, named after the First World War battle in that place.

The snowmobile had a better reception until the environmentalists got at it and succeeded in having it banned from most of our more accessible winter byways, on grounds that it was too noisy and frightened the birds and animals. For a while it appeared that the snowmobile was here to stay because people in other countries started making them and shipping them to Canada, thus appealing to our instinct that if a thing is imported, it must be good. But when the eco-nuts started getting the upper hand, and winter snowfalls got thinner, the competition fell away. Of the Asians, only Yamaha survives in the market at this writing.

In middle and upper social circles there is a tendency to look down on snowmobiles and snowmobilers as greasers, bowlers, and beer drinkers, with a few curlers thrown in, though curling cuts through the social stratas chiefly because a lot of golf clubs have rinks where men and women of means indulge. The winter fairways offer easy going for cross-country skiing. People who follow that sport regard snowmobiles as inventions of the devil, though a single snowmobile does a marvellous job of breaking trail.

The Swiss, I am told, feel somewhat the same about their own great national invention, the cuckoo clock. Most Swiss wouldn't be found dead with one, any more than they would be caught wearing digital watches.

So it was with some diffidence I announced that among the Christmas presents at our home was a second snowmobile, causing our city friends to fall down, laughing. They thought having our first snowmobile was bad enough, though they made allowances for the fact that in her role as the Hon. Member for Gatineau, my mate had to get around somehow, her riding having more snowmobile trails than the rest of the country put together, excluding only the Arctic regions. Her constituents include members of the Hill and Gully Riders, the world's biggest snowmobile club, who, garbed for the trail, resemble beings from another planet. Beneath those layers of clothing and plastic, though, most snowmobilers have hearts of gold, and getting to know them has softened my original resentments about their early encroachments onto the ski snows.

But it wasn't sentiment that led me to give my love a snowmobile for Christmas. Rather, it was the fact that no woman alive, at least none of my acquaintance, can start a pull-cord snowmobile motor when the temperature is minus 30 — or anywhere below zero. I have seen women start pullcord outboard motors in the summertime, and God knows that can be challenge enough, but it is child's play beside the sulk of an inert snowmobile when the frost is on the sparkplug and the wind is whipping up your drawers.

The Hon. Member for Gatineau has a good arm on her but try as she might at minus 30, there was no way she could get our Number One machine to catch and, at the same time, keep her hand jiggling the throttle — especially while waving at passing constituents. With my own 230 pounds of lard and sinew I could usually manage the required force, once I learned to be sure that the ignition key was turned on and that the panic button was in the right position. The panic button is coloured red with a streak of lightning through it, and you are supposed to hit it when you find yourself going over a cliff or heading for an obstacle, such as a moose, a cow, another snowmobile, or a tree. If, on starting, you don't notice it's down, you can pluck until your eyeballs come out, and it's no go.

So, the reason for the second snowmobile was that it had an electric starter on it, battery driven, as big a breakthrough as when they put starters on cars or outboards.

We refer to these things the way country people used to talk about their horses, and Madame could simply mount her new steed and at a touch of the button be off, provided the machine hadn't frozen to the ground. If frozen in, she still had the problem of lifting the back end with one hand and fiddling with the throttle with the other, hoping the drivetrack would spin and clear itself of ice. The Hon. Member managed this feat by closing her eyes and thinking of Grits, thus giving her the strength that comes of rage.

Why bother with snowmobiles at all, if we're so hot on skiing? Well, if you want to get from point A to point B, as from your parked car to your cottage with loads of supplies, the snowmobile develops a beauty of its own. I know, having tried the long trudge with a toboggan through deep snow, hellish on the upgrade and a nightmare going down — it's no wonder the pioneers drank so much.

It is a curious characteristic of Canadians that they all own, or want to own, cottages, usually referred to as "summer" cottages, overlooking the fact that the most beautiful times of the year in the Canadian countryside are autumn and winter, and even spring if you leave out the weeks of break-up. The cottage as an all-season abode has been made practical by the availability of electricity, telephones, ploughed roads, the snowmobile, and the many devices available to ensure a flow of running water — such as electrically heated pipes down into the lake, which keep the plumbing operational while they keep the meter spinning, and melt a canyon in the snow that would enable us to grow Gatineau grapefruit in January.

The snowmobile, with a device known as a ski-boose

fastened on the back, can convey passengers in great comfort, provided a fur robe is available and a cushion for the tush. And since Milady's new pushbutton snowmobile came with a fibre-glass replica of an Inuit sledge, she can haul anything up to a piano, including carting out the garbage. In her new Christmas snowmobile she moved a desk and chair (gifts to me) and assorted other items of furniture crafted in India, not to mention the full ingredients for the Christmas and New Year's dinners, and all the city water and French wine we could drink. The wine was in containers known in Quebec as "the cottagers' friend." It used to come in gallon jugs, then they cut it down to four-litre jugs, a gyp, and now they put it in cardboard dispensers lined with tinsel that you have to break open and squeeze to get the last drop — which is a chapter in itself, though not very funny.

If it's transportation you want so the cottage can be used the year around, the snowmobile is the thing — better than the horse ever was and needing less care, though you can't eat it in extremity, as the Inuit trapper said when asked why he preferred a dog team to a Ski-Doo. The biggest peril is that, having reached your destination, especially through a blizzard, you feel like celebrating with a jug of martinis, which dulls the senses for everything that is to follow, including the cross-country skiing. (Recipe for dry martinis: Procure a bottle of gin, put it in the freezing compartment of the refrigerator, and to the extent that the gin shrinks, top it up with chilled vermouth. Result: a whole bottlefull of Martinis, very dry. Refrain from putting the bottle to your lips or the stuff will freeze your innards and you will die, happily but horribly.)

So here's a non-alcoholic toast to M. Bombardier's much-maligned invention, today's version of the wonderful one-hoss open sleigh. O'er the fields we go, laughing all the way, though the sound may be drowned out by the roar of our engines.

We haven't yet figured out how to have the hot tub spa turned on before we arrive at the cottage, though I read where some people in California had it rigged up to the phone so they could call ahead and get things bubbling. Any country that solved the variable-pitch propeller should be able to come up with something.

Dem Damn Chinamen!

We knew we had a problem when the spiral staircase arrived at the cottage from Shanghai and the Quebec workmen eyed the directions for assembly, which were in English. The crate containing the staircase parts weighed 500 kilograms, which was just the start of the problem because rural Quebeckers still work by Imperial scale. We had found this out earlier when the carpenters eyed the architect's drawings for the cottage extension, all of which were worked out in metric. Cries of "Tabernacle!" and "tabernouche!" and "calice!" filled the air, but they went to work anyway, and the new parts of the cottage went forward by guess and "by God!"

We suffered through the fishing season, the bug season, and the caribou season in northern Quebec, the moose season, the deer season, and now it was the duck season, so you never knew how many people were going to turn up any day, rural workers being like Inuit when the polar bears are on the ice. The best days were the ones when there were six half-ton trucks in the yard, and the hammers were flying and the chain saws snarling away — the sight of a young male Quebecker cutting a hole in your wall with a chain saw is something you will remember always.

Problems were met, and overcome, in our two maternal languages, and things were going fairly well, which is to say without bloodshed, until the arrival of the spiral stairs. This was a staircase copied from one in the old Eddy Paper Mill in Hull, which is to Ottawa what Pest is to Buda, in the Hungarian sense. This Quebec-style cast-iron staircase was discovered by some smart interior designer in Toronto and taken apart piece by piece, and the pieces shipped across the continent and across the Pacific Ocean to Shanghai, where a foundry was found that could make moulds and turn out staircases by the hundreds. Once cast, the pieces were placed in crates and shipped to Toronto, for trans-shipment to the buyers — in our case the site was only thirty miles north of the mill in which the original staircase had stood for 100 years.

Lifting the crate was hard enough for four burly sons of the Gatineau. Prying it open was the next step, and lugging the parts inside went ahead with grunts and gasps. Finally, all was ready, and assembly commenced.

There was a long pipe to serve as the hub, and each piece had to be fitted over it at the top, and dropped down into place. The first drop would be for a distance of ten feet, which is quite a lot for a cast-iron stair plate weighing thirty-five kilograms. After each stairplate there was a riser to drop down, and a curved sidepiece, looking like Spanish lace but feeling like a block of lead. Each stair became a three-piece unit, fastened by an iron balustrade with a brass teat screwed on the bottom.

If you think this sounds complicated, you should have been there. Where you put the entrance of a spiral staircase, at the bottom, decides where the exit will come out at the top, but how can you be sure, especially when the directions were written in Shanghai, in English, and your workmen speak Quebec French? It became a matter of saving face, the Quebeckers versus the unseen Chinese, with me caught in the middle, shouting suggestions that no worker could understand.

The structure rose, like the leaning tower of Pisa, and with it rose a wooden scaffolding to prevent the whole thing from falling into the hot tub, installation of which had preceded the staircase and could be a chapter in itself. Finally, the summit was reached and the exit wasn't where it should be, which involved swivelling the whole thing around. Four sets of Quebec arms accomplished this feat of engineering, and it was time to install the brass rail that would finish the whole thing off. The directions had warned that bending the brass rail to fit the stairway would require a degree of muscle, so the men spit on their hands and set to the task.

An hour later they were still trying, but the brass rail would not yield. There were oaths aimed at the Chinois, though I suggested that part of the fault might be in Toronto. Finally, the strongest of the workers, totally frustrated, said to "Let dem damn Chinamen come over here and try by God!"

Next day, a pipe-bending machine was brought and applied to the task, without success. The rail just would not bend. Finally, six men devoted all their strength to the job, and holes were drilled in sequence, and finally the rail was in place, with only one of the cast-iron balustrades broken.

Everybody agreed it looked very pretty, but when I suggested to the men that they hang out their shingle as spiral-stair installers, they said they hoped never to see another one in their lives. And when I said the original installation at Eddy's had probably gone smoother, they admitted that erection of cast-iron staircases, like the building of the pyramids in Egypt, was a lost art. The staircase shakes a little when you come down it, but I don't dare complain, and it certainly adds a touch of class to the establishment, even though the workers said a plain ladder would have done as well.

That staircase, incidentally, serves as a reminder of the importance the Eddy Paper Mill once had in the life of the national capital. Not only did Eddy's make the money that eventually was bequeathed by the widow Eddy to Prime Minister R. B. Bennett, but it represented the only productive payroll in the country's biggest government town.

To many, myself included, it seemed useful for our legislators to have a real industry right under their noses, especially since it gave off such powerful stinks, the kind of privacy-invading effluvium that Canadians have had to live with in every mill town in the country. And there was something delightful about the big neon sign the Eddy company erected directly across the Ottawa River from the Parliament Buildings advertising White Swan toilet paper, visible by night and by day with its two enormous swans swimming gracefully along in a sea of bumph.

They say every judge should keep a roll of toilet paper under the courtroom bench as a reminder of mortality, and for years

MPs and senators had a whole factory crammed with the stuff in full view, the great vats fouling the air. One unfortunate workman fell into one of those vats and was lost in the morass, no trace of him ever being found. So they buried six boxes of White Swan tissue, amid the wails of the bereaved.

The mill site is being turned into a park and museum location, so the productivity days are gone, along with the smell. They say the stonework in the Parliament Buildings is flaking away because of acid rain from the States, but I think the damage was done in the days when toilet paper was in flower across the river.

Part of our national comedy has been played out in Hull, starting with the fact that most French-speaking residents of the place can't pronounce it, dropping the "H." Few English-speakers can pronounce it the French way, which involves pursing the lips. Nor can Anglos handle the sound of the French version of the Quebec side of the capital region, Outaouais. The Hon. Member says we can solve the whole thing by calling the region Gatineau, which everybody can pronounce. But most of what Anglos call Gatineau is actually West Hull, which is not west of Hull but north. They had a contest to rename it, and the winning entry was a combination of place names along the Gatineau River, Farrelton, Kingsmere, Burnett, Kirk's Ferry, and Gleneagle, and it came out "Farking Barkirgle." But it was discarded as not sounding French. They did rename Wakefield "La Pêche," but nobody calls it that anyway. Back to Hull.

At the height of the Quiet Revolution, when a new wave of Quebec separatism was gathering (the waves never stop, but every fifty years or so there's a big one), the Liberal government of the day decreed that the national capital of Canada was not Ottawa but Ottawa-Hull. The government of Quebec was not consulted, and offered no consent, agreeing to watch with interest while the feds flooded money into that part of Quebec lying across the river from the Parliament Buildings.

That portion of Hull once known as Sin City, because of its bars and whorehouses, was razed, and most of it was paved into superhighways that were sunk into canyons. Around and above this expanse of concrete was erected the greatest single spread of government buildings since President Juscelino Kubitschek erected Brasilia as a hinterland replacement for Rio de Janeiro. They threw a bridge across the river to link this vast complex with what Ontario people call The Mainland, and they moved 30,000 federal public servants over into the land where Champlain had portaged, and where the only legal language was French.

The idea was to charm the natives into thinking that they were, indeed, part of Canada. The immediate response of the residents of Hull was to elect a separatist, Jocylyn Ouellette, to represent them in the Quebec National Assembly. Her attitude to the $3 billion worth of new federal buildings in her constituency was that they would house the interface departments an independent Quebec would need to deal with the remnant of Canada across the river. She did stop short of proposing machine-gun nests on the new bridge.

The Hull City Council, bemused by this tidal wave of federal spending, decreed that all civil servants working in the new complexes should do so in French. But study as they would, at taxpayers' expense, Anglo civil servants seemed unable to master a working knowledge of our other maternal language, and English kept popping out of them every time they opened their mouths or put pen to paper or finger to keyboard.

The ultimate in comedy ensued when it was discovered that Hull had no sewage disposal system, dumping its raw waste into the river with no thought of pollution — thus following the example of all Quebec communities with a river nearby, including Montreal. This had always been regarded as Quebec's own business, but now, it was pointed out, civil servants who lived in Ottawa were eating their breakfasts on the Ontario side of the river, where sewage disposal facilities existed, but they were crossing to their offices in Hull, where they would evacuate or void themselves, to use the medical terminology. The Ottawa Transportation Commission threatened to refuse to carry workers from Ottawa to Hull under these conditions, urging that the Ottawa River deserved better at the hands, or more properly the bottoms, of federal public servants.

The controversy raged, and there were proposals that Ottawa-based civil servants should take potties to work with them in Hull and bring the stuff back for processing on the

Ottawa side at day's end. It was suggested that all civil servants working in Hull wear diapers, or hold their water and fecal material until they were safely home. In the end, the solution was for the federal government to build a sewage disposal system for Hull, at a cost of $100 million.

Since then, there have been claims about the renewed purity of the Ottawa River, though the sawdust of the centuries is said to be ten feet thick on the river bottom, giving off great burps and gurgles of gaseous matter, and there are suspicious-looking lumps of stuff floating in the water just off the prime ministerial residence at 24 Sussex Drive. Nobody has ever analysed this matter, but nobody swims in that vicinity, and if you have the misfortune to fall in, as I have done while sailing those picturesque waters, you get an itchy rash.

When the Eddy Mill was still in full operation across from Parliament, I once stood with the Finnish ambassador and watched its raw waste foaming into the river, and His Excellency sighed that it was a great pity.

"The pollution?" I asked.

"No," he said, "the waste. In my country, we convert that stuff into booze and drink it." He went on to explain that the Finns convert everything they can lay their hands on into strong drink, including, during the war, tables, chairs, and picture frames.

There have been a lot of jurisdictional disputes between Ottawa and Hull, and the Quebec government has yet to give its approval to any of the federal government's territorial claims. There is no legal basis for any of the federal activities on the Hull side, including the issuing of Canadian passports and the printing of government documents in the Printing Bureau, the only government building in the world with a trout stream running through its basement.

Look at your passport, citizens, and you will see that it is marked "Issued in Hull." Nobody outside Canada ever heard of Hull, and foreign passport inspectors can be thrown off by this reference to a capital that, so far as they know, does not exist. But we muddle through, and we can be thankful that, at the height of the Separatist scare, they didn't move the Mint across the river, which could have left the rest of Canada without any money.

The most recent to-do has been about where to put the huge, new waste disposal site that the capital needs, since Ottawa discharges more waste per capita than any other city in the world, if you include paper. No section of the city wanted the site, and tentative overtures to Hull and Gatineau were rebuffed without so much as a "Merci, mais non, merci." The game of garbage roulette was in full swing when, suddenly, it became known that the United States Embassy was up for grabs, the designated site on Sussex Drive having been vetoed by Washington on the grounds that it was not terrorist-proof and could be blown away by a car bomb.

In vain was it suggested that nobody in peaceful old Ottawa would want to blow away the American Embassy — rather, it was pointed out that U.S. embassies were being bombed throughout the world more often than anybody else's embassies, including the Russians. And who would ever have thought of the prime minister of Sweden being gunned down on a Stockholm street? Despite the risk, virtually all the communities that had turned thumbs down on the garbage dump wanted the new U.S. Embassy, including Hull and Gatineau.

But, alas, the one place the embassy wanted to go was in a park adjacent to the posh Village of Rockcliffe, the place with the highest per capita incomes in the land and the crumpets, tea, cocktail, and drug centre of the National Capital Region. And Rockcliffe responded to the suggestion as though it had been offered the garbage dump — which it hadn't, even though there had been a suggestion that the waste disposal site be located on Parliament Hill.

The burghers of Rockcliffe marched in protest, saying that if the U.S. Embassy located in their midst they would all be blown out of their beds when it was torched by terrorists. At time of writing this controversy still remains unresolved, and the U.S. Embassy continues in its old premises across from Parliament Hill, with a bunch of steel hitching posts sunk into the sidewalk in front so car bombs can't get too close. The government wants that building, though nobody is sure what for, the suspicion being that it will be the future location of either the Prime Minister's Office or the National Press Club bar, those being the two focal points in the running of the country.

The Living Sears

Val Sears of the *Toronto Star* is the master of the quip and the quote, his most famous having sounded the death knell of two Conservative prime ministers. The first was when he boarded the Diefenbaker campaign plane in 1963 and said: "To work, gentlemen, we have a government to overthrow." And the second was aboard the Joe Clark campaign plane in the 1980 election when Clark greeted him with the question: "How long are you going to be with us, Mr. Sears?" The reply: "Just as long as it takes, sir. Just as long as it takes."

Sears's favourite story of national funny business is the one involving Victor Mackie of the *Winnipeg Free Press* and the arrival of the Pearson entourage in St. John's, Newfoundland, at the start of the 1962 election campaign. This was in the days when the telegraph companies competed with one another for press business, even though it paid only ten cents for 100 words. They did it for the honour of the thing, as W. C. Fields used to say about being ridden out of town on a rail. The telegraph companies bootlegged, pimped, and pampered for the press corps, and they moved copy more reliably, if not more rapidly, than today's impersonal electronic gizmos do.

The telegraph company people even passed judgement on what they were called upon to transmit, as when I urged CN Telegraphs in Charlottetown to expedite a dispatch of mine and the voice at the telegraph office said if it was as good as the piece I had sent yesterday, they would get it off with all speed. Yesterday's piece had been a tribute to the late and great Blair Fraser of

Maclean's, written upon receipt of the news of his death by drowning. I doubt that the telegraph guys thought as highly of my current story about P.E.I. politics, but they sent it anyway.

Enough. Back to the famous Victor Mackie muck-up in St. John's. *Sears*:

When we got off the plane in Newfoundland with Pearson, the enthusiasts of the local constituency association handed us a press kit containing all sorts of background material, including the texts of the local speeches for that night's meeting, a text of Pearson's speech, the names of all the girls in the local band, a history of Newfoundland, and the delights of the tourist trade — the whole thing was three or four inches thick, about 300 pages.

We were also told that there would be a marvellous party for us after the speech. As usual, there was no point in explaining to the locals that immediately after the speech we would have to write, and therefore if they were going to have a party for us, they ought not to start until at least an hour or so after the meeting was over. This never made any impression, because we always wound up writing after the meeting, then going to the appointed room where all the booze was gone, the locals had gone home, and we would end up drinking whatever we had in our luggage. We never met anybody at all except each other. Among the ones who licked up the party liquor were the messengers who were waiting to collect our copy, and they invariably got bombed, as they did this time.

The man in the biggest hurry to get his copy out that night was Vic Mackie of the *Winnipeg Free Press*. He was anxious that the wires be kept open for him to get his stuff through, because the *Free Press* was hot on Pearson, as it was on all Grits in those days. As this was a suppertime meeting in Newfoundland, Mackie had a chance of catching his late edition in Winnipeg, and he had alerted his desk to stand by.

Mackie sat down at his typewriter and slammed his first take down on top of this pile of bumph the locals had handed out and called, in the mode of the times, "Boy!" The CN messenger picked up the whole pile and Mackie didn't look up, urging the movement of his copy to the telegraph office with a shouted reminder of its importance. The messenger, crazed with drink, dashed across to the office and burst upon the telegraph operator, shouting: "Get this off to the *Winnipeg Free Press*, instantly! It's from Mr. Mackie, a very important client!"

The operator, beholding the bulk of the matter placed before him, said, "Jesus! Not the whole thing?" "Don't argue!" said the messenger, mimicking the imperious tones of Mackie. "This is top priority, urgent! Very important!"

"All right," said the telegraph operator, and he pulled his eye shade down, adjusted his armbands, and locked the door of the office before tackling the pile addressed to the *Winnipeg Free Press*. He started with Mackie's lead paragraph, and then went into the text of the Pearson speech.

Out in Winnipeg the editors were awaiting Mackie's copy, and when they saw that the full text of the Pearson speech was coming through they concluded that something momentous must have transpired, and they called for the big type. The chief editor was summoned to view Mackie's dispatch, and by the time he arrived at the teletype the text of the speech had finished and the history of Newfoundland was coming through. Sensing a mishap, the editors started thumping and kicking the machine in hopes of cutting off the flow, but it kept coming, like the sorcerer's broom. The names of the girls in the band, and all the instruments they played, and the tourist attractions of Newfoundland, plus the speeches made by all the local dignitaries, and their biographies.

No other newspaper in Canada received a single word from their correspondent on the scene because the wire was jammed with the stuff for the *Winnipeg Free Press*. And that paper had not received the second take of Mackie's own dispatch because the door to the telegraph office was locked and the operator was deep in his transmission, working his way through the pile.

The rest of us, wanting to file so we could go to the party, went across the street and banged on the door of the telegraph company, but the operator, dimly perceived in the gloom within, just waved us off. When he had finished with a history of the inshore fishery, he picked up his coat and hat and left. The rest of us never did get to file, and when we sought to drown our sorrows at the party, all the booze was gone. In the *Winnipeg Free Press* newsroom Mackie's piece stretched from one end of the building to the other, and not a word of it was of any use. We heard it cost the *Free Press* $3000, which seems a lot because it would have meant 300,000 words. None of us spoke to Mackie for days afterward, and his editors weren't too keen on him either.

Thus the Mackie caper according to Sears. There are other versions, including Mackie's own, but they need not trouble us here.

Sears's story triggered my own memory about the worst day Pierre Trudeau had on his mania campaign of 1968. If you hadn't heard that Trudeau had a bad day during that triumphant campaign this story will tell you why, and again it was those rascally telegraph operators, though I have always had a suspicion that Trudeau's own handlers fixed things in their man's favour.

The day started in Halifax in a driving rainstorm. Everybody in the crowd got soaked, and Trudeau got cranky and spoke badly. On to Greenwood in the Annapolis Valley. Trudeau was late arriving, so much of the crowd had left the rally. From there we flew to Yarmouth, made a hairy landing in darkness, and again the rain kept the crowd down and Trudeau was off his form. The plane finally carried us to Chatham for a meeting in nearby Newcastle that was a flop, so we all went to our hotel rooms to write about how the wonder candidate had lost his charm and hadn't kissed a woman all day. We wondered: Had he lost his momentum? Was Trudeaumania on the way out?

We handed our copy to the CN messengers and most of us adjourned to a restaurant just outside of town where they had the first run of fresh salmon on the menu. We were well into this feast when telephone messages started arriving from our respective offices, wanting to know where the night's copy was. Not a word had been received by any paper in the country. We sent a delegation to investigate, and they returned with the news that the telegraph office was locked and all the lights were out. But one of the telegraph operators was reached at his home and he said all the copy had been dispatched, so our editors were told to be patient.

What the operator neglected to say was that he and his fellows had overimbibed, and when the torrent of press copy hit their counter they eyed it with mounting horror. A truckdriver friend en route to Fredericton stopped in for a snort, so they handed him the whole pile of copy and told him to give it to the telegraph office there. Fredericton is a good four-hour drive from Newcastle, and there is no record that the truckdriver ever made it. Certainly, the copy didn't. The result was that the stories of Trudeau's worst day never got into the paper and, since the TV guys couldn't get anything out because of the weather, it didn't make it to the airwaves either.

Next day the weather improved, and so did Trudeau's temper, and the mania started mounting again, with results that are part of our political history. That history might not have been changed had those telegraph operators done their duty, but none of us who were victimized by their dereliction has ever been sure.

You might wonder why we didn't dictate our stories over the telephone, and the answer was that we were assured the telegraphed copy was on its way. Besides, many of us had a phobia about tidings sent over the phone for publication. In our office this was known as the Bankok Syndrome, because of an incident involving transmission of one of my columns from a room in Toronto's Park Plaza Hotel.

It was at a time when they were just starting to pipe dirty closed-circuit movies into the city's top hotels, a business in which Toronto pioneered though it is now commonplace in just about every city and town in the country. I noted that one of the movies available from "room service" was *Emmanuelle*, so I phoned to have it piped up and when nothing appeared on the screen I called back to complain. I said all I was getting were diagonal lines, and when the girl asked if there was any sound I said: "Just heavy breathing." "That's all the sound there is in that movie," she chirped, and just then the picture came clear, of the heroine copulating with a fellow passenger in the washroom of an Air France jumbo jet.

When the movie was over, a dozen copulations, simulations, and masturbations later, I sat down to write an indignant column wondering what a classy hotel like the Park Plaza was doing sending dirty movies up to my room. The column finished, I phoned it through to the young receptionist in our Ottawa bureau, who took it down on her typewriter and put it out on the wire.

It was our rule in telephone transmission to spell all proper names and place names, and indicate all punctuation and paragraphing, so I did that, inserting into my story that, for the benefit of those unfamiliar with *Emmanuelle*, it was a story of high life in the diplomatic corps in Bankok. Unfortunately, the only place name in the story that I failed to spell was Bankok. I got a call in the morning from our editor, Christopher Young, telling me he had just put out the funniest correction in the long history of Southam News. It read: "In Lynch column about dirty movie in hotel room, please read place name Bankok, repeat Bankok, not bang cock, as transmitted."

And the poor girl who transcribed that dispatch and put it out was known forever after as the bang cock girl, which resulted in her career in journalism being nipped before she ever really got started.

One more from Sears: In what I think is the finest political meeting town, Port Hawkesbury, Nova Scotia, they had a church on top of a hill where the meetings were always held, and the participants used to signal their appreciation by getting up and banging their chairs on the floor, setting up a terrible racket. It meant that at a good meeting the entire assemblage would slowly inch forward and wind up crowding the speaker against the wall.

After one such meeting we press people were lucky not to get crushed by the wall of chairs, and we adjourned to our motel where the locals had set up a bar. Somehow I found myself behind the counter serving drinks. A uniformed policeman swaggered up and I asked him if he wanted a drink. He said he might have one, so I poured him a good hooker of rum and handed it to him, asking: "Sir, will you have some Coke with that?"

He drew himself up, and said: "Not while I'm on duty, sir!"

Mike Duffy, the Dastard

Electronic gizmos are so much a part of the news business that we wonder if we are running them or if they are running us. I am not talking about the computers that dominate the newsrooms, to the point where the only people using typewriters are the reporters for television and radio who have to write out their ad libs so they can read them.

Newspaper reporters now set out on assignments with almost as much gear as the electronic reporters need, though it's more portable. Portable tape recorders, portable video terminals, portable cups to snap onto telephones for transmission of copy, extension cords so plugs can be reached in hotel rooms. And, in extreme cases, portable electronic typewriters that weigh only three pounds and accomplish miracles relative to the old monsters we used to lug, except that their ribbons only work once and they need thermal paper that can only be bought in Japan.

Since I work both for newspapers and radio stations I also carry with me my portable studio, which consists of a special red telephone with microphone attachments, and alligator clips that are supposed to convert regular telephones into studio-quality transmitters, provided you know how to take the phone apart and attach the clips to its vitals. The telephone companies have been getting smarter and smarter, with the result that a lot of phones these days can't be taken apart at all, and if you can reach their insides they're different and there's no place to attach the alligator clips. By the same token, most of the fancy phones now on the market won't take the rubber bra cups that are needed for transmission from the portable video terminals, so you can wind up with all this fancy equipment rendered useless because of progress.

To complete my inventory, I have a tape transcriber that is activated by a foot pedal so I can have both hands free while turning cassette tapes into type, but this transcriber has a tendency to eat any tape inserted into it, transforming it into spaghetti. So I wind up with old-fashioned tape machines which involve pushing buttons by hand, which makes for a lot of sore fingers.

One of the early casualties of the new technology was Mike Duffy, the most readily recognizable television reporter in the world, and one of the best. Before he became famous, we used to refer to Duffy as The Porker — and since he reached the top it has been said that women will have achieved true equality when one of them who looks like Mike Duffy makes it on TV news.

Duffy wanted to tell me the story of how, as a young reporter for the radio station in Amherst, Nova Scotia, he had succeeded in getting an exclusive interview with John Diefenbaker on the campaign train from Amherst to Truro, only to have members of the national press corps plug into his tape recorder and steal the interview from him, thus robbing him of an early triumph. He was too much in awe of the Ottawa reporters to protest, an attitude he has since overcome. We both agreed that Duffy should keep that story for his own memoirs, which he promises will be forthcoming as soon as he gets a moment for contemplation of the past.

In the meantime, over a sandwich and a beer in the Press Club bar, Duffy offered his own version of the legendary occasion in which an irate husband chased him down the railroad tracks and he was saved from a cruel fate by the intervention of Pierre Trudeau. There are as many versions of this story as there were witnesses to the event, but this is right from Duffy's own mouth, though he leaves us in doubt about what the husband suspected him of doing — robbing the house, or making passes at his wife, or both. *Duffy has the floor*:

It was the 1974 election campaign, and Trudeau, harking back to Diefenbaker's 1965 campaign, decided to take the train from Sydney, Nova Scotia, to Montreal, whistle-stopping along the way. We soon discovered, we younger guys, that one of the problems of being on a train is that there are long stretches where you have no chance to get to a phone to call in your stuff.

So there we were, going along the shore of the St. Lawrence, and we came to a place called Ste-Anne-de-la-Pocatière, which at the time was in the heart of Social Credit country. Trudeau had held a press conference on board the train and had given us all kinds of stuff about all kinds of things, so I had a big package of tape to send, carefully timed so I could get it off during the ten-minute stop. By agreement, they had a whistle signal at three minutes and another one at two minutes, so any of us who were sending wouldn't miss the train — no waiting.

The problem always was to get to a phone ahead of the crowd, so in Pocatière I jumped from the train before it had stopped and ran to the nearest house, which happened to be that of the station master, adjacent to the station itself. I knocked on the door and a nice-looking woman answered. In my best Prince Edward Island French I asked if I could use the phone. She said sure, in French, but she didn't want any long distance. I waved my credit card at her and said it would be all *très bien*.

The woman was a little uncertain about this, but she shrugged and told me to go ahead. To this day, I remember how nice she looked in her white jump suit and with her hair done, all primped up to greet the Trudeaus. Senator Gil Molgat came by and I called him over and asked him to explain, and he did, and that calmed her down. The two of them walked down the platform to where Pierre and Margaret were doing their stuff, leaving the house to me.

I remember being surprised by the fact that sitting on the telephone table was a piece of mail, in French, a form letter from Oral Roberts, seeking contributions. We'd been warned by the Trudeau people that we were in Créditiste country and that there were strange and peculiar political customs in this part of the world, but I couldn't believe the hand of Oral Roberts reached so far.

I had the phone apart in no time, my alligator clips hooked on to the connections in the mouthpiece, and the transmission went well. The three-minute warning sounded, then the two-minute, and I finished and pulled the wires off, screwed the phone back together, and rushed out the door.

As soon as I hit the platform this huge man lunged at me, grabbed me by the shoulder, and wanted to know, in French, "What were you doing in my house?" Now this is where there's a bit of uncertainty, and it is possible he asked what I was doing with his wife. Whatever, he was mad as hell. Obviously, he was the station master. Just as obviously, he was the husband of the woman who had let me in.

I tried to explain, in our other maternal language, that I had just been using the telephone, and that I had the permission of his wife. He wasn't buying that at all, and by the look in his eye I could see that he suspected me of rifling either his house or his wife, while he'd been on the platform.

All of a sudden the final warning went and there were about 200 people between me and the back of the train. I shook his hand away and went barrelling down the platform, looking like 212 pounds of guilty fugitive, with the man in hot pursuit. While I was fighting my way through the crowd the train started to pull away, and I could see Pierre and Margaret waving goodbye, surrounded by Mounties and railway officials and cops with walkie talkies.

I gave chase through the crowd and broke into the open just as the train passed the end of the platform. Trudeau saw me and started to cheer. I kept pace with the train and did not gain any, but at least I had lost the husband, who was last seen remonstrating with his wife. Down the tracks we went, and I got within arm's length of the back platform when Trudeau leaned down, stretched out his hand, and I reached for it. He came within six inches of getting a grip on me to pull me up, shouting encouragement. Just at that point, the engineer threw her into high gear and the train was really moving. We wound up grabbing the air.

I have to say that in a long career with Pierre Trudeau, that was the closest we ever got — our fingers outstretched, like that image of creation by Michelangelo on the ceiling of the Sistine Chapel.

I gasped to Trudeau to go ahead, saying I'd catch him at the next stop. The old heart was pounding a mile a minute, and the breath was gone, but I turned around and started trudging back to the station, ready to face the irate husband and find a cab that might take me to the train.

Then I noticed that the people on the platform, all dressed in their Sunday best, were waving at me and shouting: "Le train! Le train!" So I looked around and sure enough, about a mile down the track, the train had stopped. Trudeau had prevailed on the railway cops with the walkie talkies to get through to the engineer and stop the train so I could catch it.

So there I was, in the worst possible situation, too pooped even to walk, and yet the prime minister of Canada was standing there waiting for me to make an appearance. So I had to turn around, gulp down a lungful of fresh air, and start back. With Trudeau watching, there was no question of walking, or ambling, or jogging — I had to run. So I ran. As I got closer, Pierre and Margaret were clapping me along and I was humping my best. Trudeau said "Come on up!" but I knew there was no way he was going to get me at close quarters in that condition, sweat-covered, dusty, out of breath, and out of shape, so I just waved.

I said thank you and ran by, found an open door and got aboard, to find Senator Molgat dictating a letter of thanks to the wife of the station master for letting this member of the media use her telephone. We staggered into the bar car, where he ordered me a cold beer and I told him what occurred.

Now I hadn't planned to file anything about this because I'm a reporter, not a columnist. I couldn't figure myself in this story. So I told it to Molgat, not noticing that some guys from the *Globe and Mail* were sitting in the next booth, listening.

We arrived in Quebec City and I filed my stuff to Toronto next day. And the office said to me: "How come you didn't file on the story of the day, which is you chasing the train. It's all over the *Globe and Mail*." And when I called home I heard the phone had been ringing all morning. In the *Globe*, Norman Webster had cast it in a kind of way that left no doubt what the husband's suspicions were.

So that's the truth of how Duffy almost got done in by his alligator clips.

"The next train I was on," said Duffy, "was the Diefenbaker funeral train, which turned out to be just as bizarre and just as full of stories — all of which I'm going to save for my own book, dammit!"

As a postscript, I told Duffy there might be an image of him on the cover of this book, along with other denizens of Parliament Hill. He came to me the next day and said he had talked it over with his lawyer and had been advised it would be bad business, so would I please see that he was not depicted.

Geez Mike, I said, Ben Wicks cartoons you all the time and it seems to be okay — this is all in fun.

"Fun for you," said Mike, his visage turned stern.

I said it was like the time we had Peter Newman playing the drums in our band for the Press Gallery Dinner Show, only to have him withdraw at the last minute on the advice of his agent. Word was it would be bad for his image on the eve of publication of his first big book, *Renegade in Power*. So Newman put down his drumsticks and we had to find a substitute, a man who could only beat time by fastening himself to the banjo player's foot.

Duffy argued that this was different, since the book was a money-making project. I had to agree that this was the intent of the work. And next day there arrived a letter on the embossed stationery of Michael D. Duffy, stating:

> This is to reiterate my request made at lunch today that my likeness NOT be included on the cover of your upcoming book, "Tales from the Press Club Bar."
>
> I am insisting on not being depicted visually in the book because it could leave the impression with the public that I had a role in writing the book, which as you know, I did not.
>
> I was pleased with your agreement today that my request will be honored.

Any time, Michael. Any old time!

MacLeod, Bejesus!

Droll stories pour out of Stewart MacLeod the way music comes out of his banjo or his fiddle, depending on which instrument he chooses to play on any given night. Properly inspired, he can do a whole hour of Nashville-style radio, climaxed by a rousing rendition of "Drop Kick Me, Jesus, Through the Goal Posts of Life."

MacLeod remembers a time when the press brigade was marooned in Saskatoon and one member, unable to contain his lust, left the hotel and threw himself into a cab, telling the driver to "take me where the women are in this town." The driver turned and said: "Repent! There is yet time to change thy sinful ways!" And he handed the wayward one a fistful of Jehovah's Witness pamphlets. The man leaped from the cab and returned to the hotel, ashen, pale, grey, and shaken. Ever since then, whenever we've needed a comic name for a law firm in a skit, we've called it that — Ashen, Pale, Grey, and Shaken.

MacLeod, after a long and distinguished career with *Weekend Magazine* and the Canadian Press, became national columnist for the Thomson newspapers, which gives him one of the widest audiences in the country.

He recalls how uneasy Mike Pearson used to be in the company of his fellow Liberal, Premier Joey Smallwood of Newfoundland. During Pearson's first campaign as Liberal leader, in 1958, he arrived in St. John's to a tumultuous welcome organized by Joey, and the two of them got into an open-topped convertible for the drive into town, through streets lined with cheering crowds. Suddenly, there was a downpour and all the crowds disappeared.

"There's no one watching," said Pearson, "let's get the top up."

Joey shook his head, rain pouring off his ample nose. "Keep waving, Mike — they'll be watching from behind the curtains."

I told MacLeod my own favourite Newfoundland story about a man from Montreal who arrived at his hotel in St. John's and took a shower, only to find there were no towels in the bathroom. He phoned down for some and was told to come and get them at the desk. He said he was dripping wet and the answer was that the floor was tiled and it didn't matter.

Next morning, at breakfast, the waitress said the cook had got drunk the night before and hadn't shown up, but that one of the maintenance men had agreed to cook breakfast.

"Fine," said the man, "I'll have poached eggs on toast."

The waitress went to the kitchen, leaving the door open, and was heard to say that a man out there wanted poached eggs.

"Poached fucking eggs!" thundered the substitute cook. And, his voice ringing through the dining room, he went on: "Who the fuck does he think he is? I can't poach fucking eggs!"

The waitress returned and asked if fried eggs would do, and in a very subdued voice the man from Montreal said yes, they would.

MacLeod has a whole raft of stories about political leaders forgetting the names of their local candidates, giving rise to the ditty: "Try to remember, the name of your member."

And I recalled the way MPs are expelled from the Commons chamber, the procedure being to have Mr. Speaker call the member's name. It can sound like a pronouncement of doom, provided the Speaker does it right. On one occasion, though, a hapless Speaker was reduced to saying: "I'd name the honourable member, if I could remember the honourable member's name!"

MacLeod recalls a Diefenbaker meeting in North Battleford, Saskatchewan, when Diefenbaker's wrath at the Liberals caused him to pound the podium with such vigour that a huge chunk of plaster left the ceiling and crashed down beside him.

Diefenbaker thundered: "Though Heaven fall, let justice be done!"

Which reminded me of a time outside Diefenbaker's office when he told the assembled reporters about a cabinet decision, and when we pressed for details he intoned: "Sufficient unto the day..." And in unison we chanted back: "Is the evil thereof!"

In Diefenbaker's closing years, MacLeod made a point of visiting him regularly in his office, and he was rewarded by being named an honorary pallbearer at Diefenbaker's funeral, an event planned, in almost every detail, by the Old Chief before he pegged out.

In MacLeod's words: I wound up with the great honour of witnessing Diefenbaker's will, until I found out that there was an army of witnesses, every time he revised the document or wrote a new one. He made it sound important and I thought I was a part of history. He got into an incredibly detailed description of the funeral train, including the fact that half the Red Ensign was going to be attached to half the Maple Leaf flag on top of his casket. He'd been told that for a state funeral the Maple Leaf flag had to be used, but he found out he could get away with using only half of it, and he chortled and said, "That'll drive the protocol people crazy." He gave the impression that he could hardly wait for the train: "By the time we get to Saskatchewan," he said, "the crowds will be coming from every direction." They did, too.

One person who got on the train along the way said he knew he was in the right place when he heard Lynch playing a lively tune on the mouth organ in one car, while Dief's secretary, Keith Martin, was crying at the other end of the train, and in the middle was Joel Aldred, roaring, "Nobody's going to tell me to fuck off on a funeral train!"

One night that I found fascinating was New Year's Eve, 1972. Pearson's body was lying in state in the Centre Block on The Hill, and I thought it would be a great atmospheric story to go out and talk to Diefenbaker, who had lived through so much with Pearson. Diefenbaker had always talked about Parliament being a Gentlemen's Club and all the camaraderie, so I thought it would be great to get him to reminisce about the happy memories, the pleasantries he and Pearson might have exchanged behind the curtains while fighting in public.

I phoned Dief, and he said it was a marvellous idea. I went out and found him with his Christmas tree and a lot of bottles of wine that had been given him, and the fireplace was going, so I pulled out my notebook and said: "Mr. Diefenbaker, you and Mr. Pearson fought for more than ten years, toe to toe, and now that his body's lying up in Parliament, you must have some pretty warm memories, sitting here tonight."

He leaned over to me and scowled. "That man," he roared, "never should have won the Nobel Prize!"

MacLeod is a founding father and leader of our National Press and Allied Workers Jazz Band, Inc., and on one occasion, when MacLeod accompanied Pierre Trudeau on an extensive global tour, we took the band out to the Ottawa airport to welcome our leader home. We brought his own banjo out there so we could hand it to him on arrival, whereupon we would strike up a few numbers.

The plane landed, and Trudeau was busy shaking hands with all his cabinet members and wellwishers, enabling MacLeod to reach us before Trudeau came by. He seized his banjo and we lit into "High Society," whereupon somebody said how good it was of us to come out to welcome the prime minister home. "Prime minister, hell," I am reported to have said. "This is for MacLeod. Let Trudeau get his own God damn band!"

Whereupon Trudeau came by and, failing to recognize MacLeod as one who had been in his company for the whole of the tour, stuck out his hand and said: "Nice of you to come out to greet me." MacLeod was speechless, but played his banjo with renewed ferocity. Health permitting, he has continued to do that at every opportunity, interspersed with outbursts of fiddling, Cape Breton style. And, as befits a son of the manse, he sometimes punctuates his music with shouts of "Come to Jee-saws!"

My kind of a columnist, MacLeod.

Down Under

Something about the Antipodes does strange things to visiting Canadian politicians, and some good stories result.

There was the time, during John Diefenbaker's round-the-world tour, when a big reception was held in Canberra, hosted by the Australian Governor General, Field Marshal Sir William Slim, 1st Viscount, the great Aussie war hero. In the Canadian entourage was Diefenbaker's brother, Elmer, the rustic member of the family whom Dief adored. Elmer was circulating through the throng at the reception and he approached the host, asking: "What's your name?"

"Slim," came the crisp reply.

"Put 'er there, Slim! My name's Elmer."

Ian MacDonald, then of the *Vancouver Sun*, recalled Pierre Trudeau's 1970 visit to New Zealand. In Trudeau's first speech in Wellington he managed to insult two of the country's greatest icons. He said: "Well, of course, the whole world knows about your very famous Black and Tans..." And there was the longest pause, amid groans, while Trudeau searched his mind for the correct name of the Rugby team, of which he obviously had never heard. He seemed to know it was black, so he tried "Black and Whites." Commotion. He was about to blurt out "Browns" when somebody mumbled in the background, "All-Blacks" — and Trudeau said it and the crowd roared.

He did the same with Sir Edmund Hillary, the conqueror of Everest. He got the Sir Edmund out, but couldn't remember the rest until, again, a voice prompted from behind, and he said it, amid cheers.

And the host, Prime Minister Sir Keith Holyoake, got into the spirit of the occasion by welcoming Trudeau with flowery references to Pacific Rim ties, Commonwealth ties, parallel histories and all that, winding up with the words: "While we share many advantages, we also have some common problems. We have the Maoris, and you have the French Canadians."

On to Christchurch, more English than Canterbury, where Trudeau watched an exhibition Rugby game at a very British-style private school. At the end of the game the players of the two teams lined up for inspection, and Trudeau passed down the line, shaking hands. Assembled nearby were the contestants in the Miss New Zealand contest, and when he had finished with the athletes Trudeau continued his inspection march through the beauty queens, kissing each of them with a passion seldom seen in New Zealand. It made all the papers.

MacDonald's mention of the Everest expedition reminded me of the lecture tour undertaken by the commander of the record-breaking climb, Sir Vivian Fuchs. Sir Vivian was appearing on a platform in the British Midlands and the chairman called the meeting to order, proceeding with a few remarks about the distinguished explorer. "Sir Vivian Fucks," he said, "is the man really responsible for the conquest of Everest. His planning was meticulous, and made it possible for the summit to be achieved by Hillary and Sherpa Tenzing. It gives me great pleasure to present to you, Sir Vivian Fucks."

Afterward, the chairman asked a friend if his introduction had gone well, and the reply was that it had, but that he should know that Sir Vivian pronounced his named "Fooks", not "Fucks."

"I know," said the chairman, "but you'd no expect me to pronoonce that word in pooblic!"

MacDonald subsequently went to work for Trudeau. One of his duties in the Prime Minister's Office was to write the PM's speech for the Press Gallery Dinner, a speech consisting of one-liners and gags with punch lines, at which Trudeau was famously bad. So MacDonald hit on the idea of writing gags on two pages — the build-up on one page, and the punch line on another. That should have resulted in the essential pause that Trudeau never seemed able to manage, to get the laugh. "But damned if he didn't master the art of page turning," MacDonald recalls, "and flipped over without missing a beat, droning the punch line and missing every laugh. And afterwards he asked me what was supposed to be funny about the speech."

Trudeau's wayward way with names was the despair of his aides, even during the Trudeaumania election of 1968. MacDonald recalls a rally in a neighbourhood ball park in Toronto where the Liberal candidates were assembled, and Trudeau was introducing them to the crowd, never having met any of them before in his life.

After getting through most of the names without mishap, he said: "And of course, I really want you to vote for my very good friend, Danny Manson."

Titters in the crowd.

"Farney Banson?"

More laughs.

So Trudeau decided to play it for all it was worth, and said: "Blarney Flamson?"

"Farley Blamson?"

Danson was hearing all this, not sure whether to laugh or cry, but the crowd loved it. It was one of the things Trudeau could get away with in the 68 campaign. Barney Danson won, and became one of Trudeau's most trusted cabinet ministers.

Both MacDonald and I were present on an occasion in Lahr, at the all-ranks mess on the Canadian Forces Base, when the then minister of national defence, James Richardson, was being introduced to the crowd. The sergeant doing the introducing gave it a real flourish when he said: "I am proud to present to you the minister of national defence, the Right Honourable Richard Jamieson!"

It was on his return from this trip that Richardson was interviewed aboard the armed forces Boeing and made his famous quote about Canada's native people having been so primitive they couldn't even invent the wheel, dragging loads, rather, on two sticks. Forevermore the minister was dubbed "Jimmy Two Sticks."

MacDonald is the man with whom I have trouped onstage from Glace Bay to Kelowna. He is the author of some of our most enduring satires and lampoons, the most memorable of which is the one he did about the parliamentary streaker, the MP who was caught in the act in his office on The Hill when a messenger entered without knocking. The messenger fled, with the MP in hot pursuit urging silence, whereupon his partner locked the office and wouldn't let him back in. It got a lot of press at the time.

The song, to the tune of "My Favorite Things," goes:

On Parliament Hill all the folks are a-gogging,
Because an MP went jigging, not jogging,
A nooner, as soon as the lunch bell went ding,
That was his kick and his favourite fling.
This is a story so full of embarrassment,
But there's no question of sexual harassment.
From what we know and as far as it went,
She was a consenting con-stit-uent!

'Twas a big fuss, interruptus
Of stolen office joys,
When a messenger happened to open the door,
Well she really knew the score!
Off down the hallway the messenger went winging,
He followed on, external affairs swinging,
Crying: "Don't tell them I'm in a jam,
"I could be snitched on by Fotheringham!"

Now hear the leaders make their disavowals,
They can't have their caucuses wrapped up in towels,
And people were wondering who can it be,
A Liberal, a Tory, or an N.D.P.?
There's a moral to this story
That has swept The Hill,
Be a liar, a phoney, a snake in the grass,
But never be caught
BARE ASS!

And MacDonald would end by assuring audiences that, whoever it was (and Fotheringham DID snitch), it wasn't Stanley Knowles.

A Little Dinner Music

Pierre Trudeau calls it "that God-damned dinner." This year, in response to an invitation, he said there was no trip he wouldn't take in order to avoid attendance, and he went to China. Through the years, the Press Gallery Dinner has seen fisticuffs and the pelting of the Governor General with buns and sugar cubes, in return for which Ed Schreyer threatened to kick a tormentor in the ass.

The speeches by the prime minister, the leader of the opposition, and the Governor General are deemed to be off the record. The songs that are sung are in the public domain, and it has often been suggested that they be bound and published, as part of our national heritage.

Here's a sampler, and it helps if you know the tunes.

In 1974 the energy minister was Don Macdonald, and he was named Man of the Year by the Toronto *Globe and Mail*. He sat for Rosedale, and he warred with Alberta, and we sang, to the tune of "Delta Dawn":

> In his Osgoode days they called him Thumper Don,
> The biggest mouthpiece you ever laid eyes on,
> He's the prickliest thorn in the roses of Rosedale,
> And the pick of the year to those pricks at the *Globe and Mail*.
> Hey! Thumper Don,
> What's that crisis you got on?
> Has that oil and gas you're sniffing got you high?

And did I hear you say,
You're gonna be PM some day
According to your pipeline in the sky!

And we had the Sheik of Saskabush, Premier Allan Blakeley, sing back at Thumper, to the tune of "The Desert Song":

Saskatchewan's calling,
Come, sink one in me.
My bushland is bawling,
Rich we will yet be,
Rolling in jewels and dough,
Oil is what's making us go!
Black, gorgeous petroleum,
And gas, seeping from every bum,
A whole machine, running on vaseline,
We've got people stinko,
On royalties, Pinko!
Oh, rapeseed and potash too,
Will bring riches for me and you,
So put your vagina, in old Regina,
And screw, hoo! hoo!

And Peter Lougheed, the Blue-Eyed Sheik of Alberta, was made to sing a ditty that we subsequently performed in his presence; whereupon his wife, Jeannie, invited me to bare my navel and into it she thrust a rhinestone, which to the best of my knowledge is still in there. Don Getty, Lougheed's successor as premier of Alberta, wondered recently when we were going to have a song about him — and we said as soon as he did something. Meanwhile, we would keep singing the Lougheed song, to the tune of the "Sheik of Araby":

I'm the Sheik of Calgary,
These sands belong to me.
Trudeau says they're for all.
Into my tent he'll crawl (like Algeria did it to de Gaulle).
The gas we've got today
We just won't fart away! (Fart away, fart away, fart away)
Gas pains don't worry me,
I'm the Sheik of Calgary!

These sands are black as pit,
I tell you bastards, shit!
And from my camel seat
I humped old Trudeau neat.
We need the industry —
We can't get none from DREE,
Albertans will be free
With the Sheik of Calgary.

To Trudeau I say, Pshaw!
He's eunuch in my casbah.
Our motive's strictly greed.
We call it our Stampede (Hitler had his panzers, I got belly
danzers).
The wagons make you chuck up,
But until we get our buck up,
It's all a fonstrous muck up,
Says the Sheik of Calgary!

In performing this song to various audiences during the years
we would ask if they wanted the clean or dirty version, and
almost always they wanted the dirty, so the lines about "fonstrous muck up" usually got enriched. But at least the clean
version introduced the word "fonstrous" into the language as a
socially acceptable epithet of moderate strength.

During the FLQ crisis, when Ottawa swarmed with soldiers
standing on guard, we did a tune to the music of "Lili Marlene,"
sung by the troops outside Rideau Hall:

Underneath the lamplight, by the Rideau Gate
Lurking in the bushes, we gun our cocks and wait
(Interjection by Sergeant-Major: "No, you silly buggers!
Not Gun your cocks! It's Cock your guns!")
Now comes our moment, tenderly,
The girls of Rockcliffe serve us tea,
And roll us in the lamplight,
And lay us in the lane!

Just across from Rideau Gate is 24 Sussex, and the famous
swimming pool, so in the 1975 show we sang, to the Labatt
commercial:

When you're Trudeau
We'll give you dough
To build your swimming pool.
It's no crass dole
For some Asshole,
It's deductible, you fool.
In his garden, he swims in the sun,
So beg your pardon, let's join in the fun,
Let it all hang, it's a gang bang,
Down at Trudeau's pool!

And there was another pool song that contained a memorable line, because it hit three targets in one breath. See if you can find it, to the tune of "Marching Through Georgia":

Round the good old swimming pool we'll sing another song,
Send the contributions in to help Trudeau along,
Dredging out a waterhole to prove the land is strong,
Let's all go swimming with Trudeau!
The pool! The pool!
It's like the golden rule,
To others do, as they would do to you!
With our PET we all get wet,
Here in the Sussex slough
Let's all go swimming with Trudeau!

(If you spotted the third line in that ditty, take a bow. "Dredging" referred to the Harbourgate scandal in Hamilton, "waterhole" is the English translation of Trudeau, and "The Land is Strong" was the slogan of the Trudeauites, rejected by John Turner, who quit. Neat-o, eh?)

In 1976, three years before he became prime minister, we did a job on Joe Clark, to the anthem of Disney's "Mouseketeers":

Who's the leader Tories picked to put Trudeau away?
J-O-S, E-P-H, C-L-A-R-K!
Who's the kid in Stornoway, the junior Sir John A?
J-O-S, E-P-H, C-L-A-R-K!
Joseph Clark! (Joe McTeer!)

Joseph Clark! (No! McTeer!)
Peaking just like Rocky Mountain high (High! High! High!)
Who's the new Albertan leaves us freezing in the dark?
J-O-S, E-P-H, C-L-A-R- CLARK!

In 1978 the Tories on Parliament Hill were complaining that their offices were being bugged, and the loudest voice was that of Elmer MacKay, even then plotting the reinvention of Brian Mulroney. MacKay's office was swept without any listening devices being found, so to "Elmer's Tune" we sang:

Why are the plants always bleeping and creeping around?
Why should the ashtray be leaping a foot from the ground?
What makes the Speaker a seeker of phones that go boom?
It's just Elmer's room.
Why does it mutter and sputter, that bucket of ice?
And is that golf bag and putter a listening device?
That old decanter and planter's a microphone boom
Live in Elmer's room.

Listen! Listen!
There's not much we're liable to be missin'
Memos, stenos, all are laid bare for General Dare,
They're drinking gin electronic, and sonic White Horse,
And there's a bottle of tonic transmitting in Morse,
The voltage bends a credenza and blows up a broom,
All in Elmer's room!

Listen! Listen!
There's not much we're liable to be missin'
Memos, stenos, all are laid bare for General Dare,
What is that static, erratic, that's filling the air?
Why does that buzzing, emphatic, resound in the chair?
You put your tush in the cushion, and you go VAROOM!
Whoopee! In Elmer's room!

(The head of the Secret Service at the time was the marvellously named General Michael Dare.)

The security chief of the day was Robin Bourne, and when a Soviet nuclear-powered satellite crashed in the Northwest Territories we sang, to the music of the "Mountains of Mourne":

Now Robin Bourne sent up his troopers to see
What our northland resembled all filled with debris.
As they picked up the pieces they tingled my dear,
And they all underwent transformations so queer!
For all that now ails them there isn't a cure,
And I don't think that we should be feeling secure.
Because of mutations, I'm sorry to see,
That the troopers of Bourne now sit down to pee!

When the Mounties set fire to a barn in Quebec, saying they did it to smoke out the terrorists, we dusted off "Hot Time in the Old Town" and sang:

One dark night, when the frogs were all in bed,
Our red coats took a torch into the shed,
Burned the stable, winked their eye and said,
There'll be a hot barn, in the old town tonight.
They all flee in flaming disarray,
Terrorists, and Panthers black and grey,
Charred and smoked, Oh! What a happy day!
We burnt a hot barn in the old town that night!

In 1980 we put Transport Minister Jean-Luc Pepin to the music of "Casey Jones" and sent him down the line:

He thinks you find grasshoppers in a hopper car,
And he says he's gonna double-track the CNR.
And all he knows of farmers is to kick them in the ass,
And he wouldn't know an airline from the Crowsnest Pass!
Jean-Luc! A-steamin' and a-strokin'
Jean-Luc! Got his caucus in his hand,
Jean-Luc! Mounted in the cab'net,
A-comin and a-goin' to the promised land!

And just in case any of you can hum "Finiculi, Finicula," try a stanza of the song we called "The Barber of Neville." A few words of explanation will suffice. Joe Clark's leadership was under stress in 1981, so his chief adviser, William Neville, sent to Toronto for a hairdresser named Umberto from the salon known as Numero Uno to come and cut Joe's hair so his ears would fit better. The bill for the trip was $300, high for a haircut in those days. You also need to know that Trudeau was getting bald, and that his principal adviser was Jim Coutts, and his hairdresser was Rinaldo. Ready? All sing:

My name, it is Umberto, I am the barber,
I send-a da bill, to Billy Ne-ville.
In hair, the boys all call me Numero Uno,
I make-a- da clip,
Three hundred a trip.
Forget, about this fellow called Rinaldo,
The so-and-so, who does Trudeau.
Who cares? There really isn't that much hair there,
There's too few roots,
And too many Coutts!
Joe Clark! Joe Clark!
There's a head of fuzz!
Clip it! Snip it!
Make it slick because,
Because, because, because, because,
Because, because, Be-Cause!
Joe who, and what, and why, and when
Must not become Joe Was!

The repeal of the Crow's Nest Pass grain rates gave rise to a ditty sung by the western premiers, addressed to Jean-Luc Pepin to the tune of "Bye Bye Blackbird":

If you want to move a pile
Half a cent a ton a mile
Don't call Pepin!
Now you've killed the status crow
How about some quid pro quo,
Jean-Luc Pepin?
Monsieur Pepin's acting like a true Grit
All that he can haul's a load of bull shit
We would like to kick his ass
Right across the Crowsnest Pass
Pepin! Bye bye!

We used the "Battle Hymn of the Republic" over and over, the last time to sing the praises of the Mulroney Sacred Trust Company, swearing to keep the social programs intact. The singer, Ian MacDonald, was dressed as His Holiness the Pope, known as J2P2:

> You should do your banking with Mulroney's Sacred Trust,
> Endorsed by J2P2, the Pope who knows no lust.
> The interest rate ain't very great, but it never will go bust.
> Like Wilson, you should save, you should save!
> Universality forever!
> Change the social programs? Never!
> The rich and poor will hang together
> With money from the Sacred Trust!

The Mulroney anthem, "Humble," was so familiar we used the original words, and then followed them with:

> O Lord! It's hard to be humble
> When you've got such a wonderful chin,
> But it only gives me one problem,
> I can't keep the damn thing tucked in.
> I've won all the seats in the Commons,
> My charisma has charmed them, you see,
> It's not every clown that can shut down a town
> And wind up a hero, like me!

Another song that required little doctoring was "You're Just in Love," when we applied it to New Brunswick Premier Richard Hatfield, singing a duet with RCMP Commissioner R. H. Simmonds:

> I hear singing and there's no-one there,
> I smell blossoms and the trees are bare,
> All day long I seem to walk on air,
> I wonder why? I wonder why?
> I keep tossing in my sleep at night,
> And what's more I can't recall the flight.
> Stars that used to twinkle off and on
> Are tinkling in my john,
> I wonder why?

(Simmonds)

> This bag needs analysing,
> It's a bit compromising,

What he took with him to the plane.
We've all heard chitter chatter
About Dick's foreign matter,
And the Queen don't need acid reign.
I am not autocratic
But I don't need the static,
If he calls Elmer, that's taboo!
When he says to Chuck and Di,
It's the only way to fly,
What the hell's a cop to do?

Through the years, we sang about the New Democratic Party, to the tune of the "Mocking Bird":

Listen to the N-D-P (coo! coo!)
Listen to the N-D-P (coo! coo!)
We are marching from the cradle to the grave!
Listen to the N-D-P (coo! coo!)
Listen to the N-D-P (coo! coo!)
Oh our party it is fading fast away!

And we paid our disrespects to the Créditiste Party, whose leader, Réal Caouette, had said that his prewar heroes were Benito Mussolini and Adolf Hitler. The tune was the "Mexican Hat Dance," and it was sung in dervish fashion, à la Caouette:

I'm Caouette, I'm the leader of Socreds,
And some Socreds is better than no creds,
And I've got no damn use for them doughheads
Who would rather be dead than Socred!
(repeat)
When they say that our party is greenie
And our Members of Parliament weenie,
I just tell them about Mussolini,
And Adolf! Mein Fuehrer! Sieg Heil!
(repeat opening)
Tell them they've nothing to lose! (clap, clap!)
Tell them you'll buy them all shoes! (clap, clap!)
Bribe them with money and booze! (clap, clap!)
Social Credit is right for today!
I'm Caouette, I'm the leader of Socreds

And some Socreds is better than no creds,
And I've got no damn use for them doughheads
Who would rather be dead than Socred!
Sieg Heil! Sieg Heil! Sieg Heil! Yaaaay!

For Premier Brian Peckford of Newfoundland we picked the
tune of "I's the Bye," concluding:

I'll come up to Ottawa,
That's my winning ditty.
How can I run Newfoundland
With fug-all in the kitty!

That came after our version of the Newfoundland National
Anthem, or the Ode, including what we called our national
unity verse:

On our big dam in Labrador
There's no bilingual poop,
No parlez-vous, for if they do
We'll pee in their pea soup!

Part of the formula was to insult all segments of political
society, and indeed of society as a whole, in equal measure —
the way media ladle out election coverage to the contending
parties in measured amounts.

Our most spectacular effort at equal insult was in a song
about the trouble eastern Canadian ears had in getting used to
some of the western names that came into prominence after Joe
Clark's election victory in 1979. Subsequently, after the Liberals got back into power, we were asked to perform at a
gathering organized by multiculturalism minister Jim Fleming.
Fleming was late arriving, and when he walked in, delegates
from all across the country heard these lines, to the tune of "You
Are My Sunshine":

Now Wasps and Frenchmen, and all their henchmen,
Don't run our national affairs.
It's us newcomers, we're Joe Clark's plumbers,
We've got you by the short hairs!

We've got Paproski, and Mazankowski,

And Konahowski, and Pope John Paul.
This is the hour, for Hunkie power,
It's Slobbovia, over all!

There's Hunkies, Pollocks,
Bohunks in sweat socks,
There's Ukes, and Krauts, and Spics, and Wops,
And in addition, there's Ray Hnatyshyn,
Garlic gas that never stops!

Higher and higher,
Mit Eddie Schreyer,
Come on, let's all get in the game,
You could be famous, though ignoramus,
If an eyechart is your name!
(Chorus) We've got...

And then there was the song about the Johnson fags. This whole show was about broadcasting and bilingualism, including an indictment of language commissioner Keith Spicer for being "cunningly lingual." Al Johnson was the president of the CBC and some of their programs were thought, by the standards of the time (1977), to be slanted toward the emerging gay community. The tune was "The Johnson Rag":

Yoo hoo! We are the Johnson fags.
It's true, we are the Johnson fags.
For you, we wear our gladdest rags,
True blue! We swallow all your gags!
C'est vrai, we really are au fait,
Olë! We're ready come what may,
Oiveh! We do it any way,
Go round the world with the Johnson fags.
People say we're queer and gay,
But overcome we shall,
We don't care what MPs say,
We've got our pal — we've got Big Al!
Yoo hoo! We are the Johnson fags,
For you, we wear our gladdest rags,
It's true, we're happy with our bags,
Creatin' and fellatin' with the Johnson fags!

My Own Brucie

During the Pearson years, when the Ottawa air was full of what Richard Gwyn called the "Smell of Scandal," we did our Press Gallery Dinner Show around the theme of RCMP commissioner George McClellan, who was forced by Pearson to cough up the secret files on members of the Diefenbaker cabinet.

There was a suspected spy in Vancouver named George Victor Spencer, and when he complained of police harassment Prime Minister Pearson telephoned him to ask if he was being treated fairly. We did a song to the tune of the "Indian Love Call," titled McClellan's love song to the spies:

> When I'm chasing you, hoo hoo hoo, hoo hoo hoo,
> Will they follow through, hoo hoo hoo, hoo hoo hoo!
> Or will the PM continue prone, and telephone,
> To ask the spies if they're happy guys,
> And leave me all alone?
> I've got files on you, hoo hoo hoo, hoo hoo hoo!
> Some of them are red, some of them are quite blue...

And so on — the whole mess wound up in the Munsinger case, which is part of our history.

Anyway, we were doing our show with a Mountie motif, and one member of the cast was the columnist for the Thomson newspapers, Farmer Tissington. Farmer, for that was really his Christian name, was the tallest man ever seen in Ottawa, standing an estimated seven feet in his socks, pre-metric. He was built to scale, so when we went looking for a Mountie uniform to put on him for the show, Malabar's, the costume people, had to let out a special contract, but they came through with the outfit, red coat and all, looking more like a marquee than a suit.

The Gallery show comes at the end of the dinner and the drinks, with the result that both cast and audience are usually well lit up for the theatrical proceedings. So it was that we got Tissington into his Mountie outfit and had him poised in the wings, awaiting his cue to go onstage. He had just one line in the show — all he had to do was walk on, face the audience, and sing: "Oh, Rose Marie, I love you!" Then stand silent for the rest of the skit.

The cue came, and Tissington didn't move. Several cast members gave him a shove and he lurched out in full view of the audience — Pearson, Vanier, Diefenbaker, the cabinet, the lot.

He stood dazed, then his lips moved, and in a voice filled with anguish, asked: "What was that broad's name again?"

Pandemonium.

The only moment in our theatricals that ever approached Tissington's triumph was the night we had Bruce Phillips, of CTV, playing Robert Stanfield, with Iain Hunter of the *Ottawa Citizen* piping him onto the stage. That was the year of Trudeau's swimming pool, and we had constructed a pool in the Railway Committee Room, where the show took place, and filled it with 17,000 gallons of water. Mr. Speaker Lucien Lamoureux, aware that the main computer room for Parliament was located directly below, viewed the whole proceedings with considerable unease.

The pool was one of those circular jobs with walls of corrugated metal, and a plastic liner, and it jiggled even without anybody in it, but we told Mr. Speaker there was no danger of collapse. Sears, who supplied it on loan, guaranteed it.

Came time for the Stanfield skit, and the wail of Hunter's pipes could be heard in the corridor outside the big room. Into the hall strode Hunter, followed by Phillips in his Stanfield get-up. Amid cheers, they made their way to the stage, and Phillips took his place at the microphone to sing his parody of "Farewell to Nova Scotia." Hunter, still piping fiercely, started backing offstage and, with Phillips clearing his throat for his opening notes, Hunter toppled backwards into the pool, the pipes blaring bubbles as he disappeared from view.

Phillips said later he had heard of being upstaged, but this was the first time he was ever downstaged so thoroughly. A roar went up from the audience as Hunter made the biggest splash ever seen or heard on The Hill.

I was standing beside the pool and watched Hunter descend to the bottom, setting up a wave that caused the walls of the pool to tremble violently, threatening to unleash a torrent that would have engulfed the nation's finest, not to mention millions of dollars of computer equipment below. The walls held, and I reached down for Hunter, who emerged, spluttering and cursing, from the depths. We lifted him out to a standing ovation, but he was in no mood for bows — he grasped his sodden pipes and squelched his way backstage, vowing never to pipe again. But he put the pipes on a radiator and they dried out and he played them in the show reprise next day, omitting the plunge.

For Phillips, this was his second brush with disaster in the Gallery show. Years earlier, during the Diefenbaker days, he staged our first massive extravaganza, keyed to Diefenbaker's Northern Vision.

Phillips arranged with the Department of Northern Affairs to turn the Railway Committee Room into a northern wonderland, with styrofoam igloos, artificial snow, electronic aurora projections, a herd of live reindeer and, to cap it all, a musk ox, which would be led into the hall at the height of the pre-dinner drinking. Everything went well and people oh'd and ah'd at Phillips's showmanship, though Mr. Speaker Michener was uneasy about the sacred halls being turned into an animal farm.

When the moment for the musk ox arrived, Phillips called for silence, but nothing happened. "Bring on the effing ox!" he roared, but still no sign. Finally, a message from the floor below — the goddam musk ox was too big for the freight elevator, and refused to climb the stairs. They were putting it back in the truck and taking it to its quarters at the Experimental Farm.

Phillips was inconsolable, and was little comforted when told by experts that, had they got the musk ox upstairs, they in all likelihood never would have got him down again. Musk oxen, like cattle, would refuse to go down stairs, though nobody could be sure, no musk ox ever having tried.

Diefenbaker made a wistful speech that night, defending his Northern Vision against the fun we poked at it — his theme being that a man's visions are worthy of respect. In this, as in his later opposition to nuclear weapons for Canada, Diefenbaker was decades ahead of his time.

Bruce Phillips was my most memorable colleague. In my view he was the best writer ever to grace the halls of Parliament, capable of prose that came close to poetry while remaining good, lean journalism. He went on to television where he made a fine name, but his true talents seldom came through because he needed lots of room and space for his best stuff, and you only find that in print. Phillips was moody and reckless with his talents, and the publishers who sat in judgement on our news service were more inclined to look at his perceived shortcomings than his obvious assets. Every time he fell into the pit of their criticism he would write his way out, beautifully. As his chief I aged visibly, but never stopped loving him for his best work, nor ever will.

My most trying time with Phillips came when he went to Quebec City to cover a crisis in the affairs of the Union Nationale government of the time, the heirs to Maurice Duplessis. Duplessis had died in September 1959, and his place was taken by the charming, captivating, knowledgeable Paul Sauvé, whose tragic death in January, after only 100 days in office, threw the province and the country into turmoil, so high had been the hopes for Sauvé's government.

The question was, who would now succeed Sauvé?

Phillips phoned me from Quebec City in the middle of the night, out of breath, and said he had the news exclusively — the successor as premier of Quebec would be Antonio Barrette, and the news would be official later in the day. "I'll file the story now," he panted, "you get out an Ottawa reaction piece and we'll have it to ourselves!"

I asked him if he were sure, and he said it was absolutely on, and not to worry. Barrette was the little-known minister of labour in the Duplessis and Sauvé governments, and his name

I join the Northwest Territories crew in the Great Centennial Canoe Race. Everybody's paddling but me, in the great tradition of the white explorers. Dave Palangio, *North Bay Nugget*.

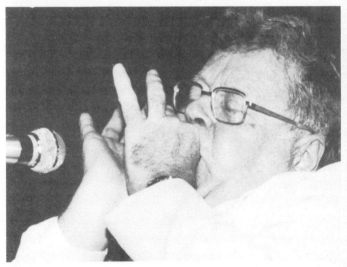

A blow note, obviously. The cheeks sink in on the draw. Brian Gavriloff, *Edmonton Journal*.

Conductor Mitch Miller wonders how he ever got into this. He's with Fred Davis and me, onstage with the Winnipeg Symphony. Photo by David Portigal.

Great moments at the National Press Club: Governor General Georges Vanier dons his Press Club tie, while John Diefenbaker looks on. Years later, given the same tie, Pierre Trudeau pretended to hang himself with it, and lied about how he always wanted to join the club. Dominion Wide and Canapress.

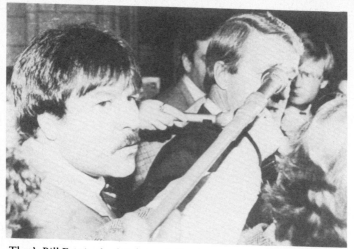

That's Bill Fox in the foreground. From the look of him, you could never be sure whether he was guiding Mulroney or holding him hostage. Canapress photo.

A word in the PM's ear from my love, Claudy Mailly, the Hon. Member for Gatineau. Years before, reading that Mailly aimed to be prime minister, lawyer Mulroney phoned from Montreal and said he'd be her bagman. She promised she'd see he got a Senate appointment. Photo by Bill McCarthy.

Press Club trio, 1986. My camera-shy daughter, Cindy Boucher, with father and an unidentified Irish baritone, doing "Irish Eyes" at 3 A.M. on Gallery Dinner night. Photo courtesy Ray Stone.

Playing out the Gary Cooper fantasy: Lynch in an impersonation of the Hon. Jake Epp, the Mennonite Mauler from Manitoba, defending the social programs in 1985. Photo courtesy Ray Stone.

My all-time favourite Gallery Dinner photo. Peter Desbarats as Pierre Trudeau, Bill Grogan as David Lewis, singing "There Will Never Be Another You" in the 1973 show we called "We're all in bed with Trudeau, and it's fun, fun, fun!" Photo courtesy Bill Brennan.

Bruce Phillips, on stage with an RCMP horse's ass, singing about the night the horsemen burned the barn. That show gave us a chance to say "horseshit" twenty-five times, bringing charges from the finicky of extreme scatology.

Dr. Eugene Forsey, caught in a rare moment of tranquility, awaiting ignition.

Senator Finlay MacDonald, OC, the laird of Chester, N.S., immaculately clad and glass in hand, "the way I'd like to be remembered." Most bagmen are shorter and fatter.

The most glamorous war correspondent, Matthew Halton (though Lionel Shapiro might have insisted *he* was).

A flush of old WCs — Walter Cronkite, myself, Ross Munro, and Bill Boss recall days together as war correspondents, and I signal how we faced death together three times in a single morning, before breakfast, in the winter of 1944.

hadn't figured in any of the speculation about the succession, so I was uneasy. But such was my faith in Phillips that I dressed and drove to the office and knocked out a piece about Ottawa's astonishment at the prospect of Barrette as premier. I filed the reaction piece with the telegraph company, and waited for word from Phillips. Nothing came. Eight A.M., and no word. Nine o'clock. Ten o'clock.

We still had afternoon papers then, papers that actually were printed in mid-day and beyond, and the phone started ringing, with editors saying my reaction piece was very interesting, but where was the news? The wires had nothing, and there was no word from any quarter.

I kept ringing Phillips's room at the Château Frontenac, but there was no answer.

Eleven o'clock, and I had to act. With sinking heart I typed out the dreadful dispatch, with a Quebec City dateline and Phillips's name on it, saying that the new premier of Quebec would be a total stranger by the name of Antonio Barrette. I padded it with the bits of background I could find of Barrette, going heavily on Sauvé and Duplessis, and away it went. Our papers had their exclusive, in large type.

Still no word from Phillips.

Finally, at five o'clock in the afternoon, came a call. An hour before, the wires had carried the news that the elite of the Union Nationale Party, in secret conclave and to everybody's complete astonishment, including their own, had picked Antonio Barrette as the new party leader and premier of Quebec. This was Phillips calling.

"What happened?" I asked, with trembling voice.

"Charlie," said Bruce, "this is bigger than all of us. I couldn't call because I was kidnapped and held in a locked room with a bucket over my head and men were beating on it with sticks and chains and it was horrible."

I asked him if he needed help, if I should rush to his side, or call the police, or what. Did he need medical attention?

No, he said, it was all over now, and he would recover, and he was sorry about not being able to file.

I told him it was okay, that we had our news beat and it was good work.

So it was, as far as it went, and to this day I have never found out where Phillips got the news, or what really happened after his never-to-be-forgotten phone call — the one call, he said, that his captors would let him make.

Phillips did this to me one other time, when we sent him to South Africa and he filed a series of dispatches that foreshadowed everything that has occurred in that unhappy country since, and this was twenty years ago. The air was filled with cheers for Phillips's performance, and a series of congratulatory cables went off to him in Johannesburg, but from his end there was only silence. No word for a week. Two weeks. Three weeks. Finally, a phone call to say he was ready to come home. When I asked what had happened, he said it was bigger than all of us, but that he was okay. Some day, he would tell me. He never has.

When Phillips was covering the Diefenbaker campaign in 1963, Mrs. Diefenbaker took a scunner to him and told her husband that he should refuse to carry Phillips on the campaign plane. Phillips was informed of his dismissal and called me for instructions. He was told to stay with it and insist on having the Southam seat on the plane, and that he should write a piece about his problem, which he did. This led to a celebrated Al Beaton cartoon in the *Toronto Telegram* showing Phillips standing outside a telephone booth, trailing a parachute, with the Diefenbaker plane disappearing in the distance.

Whatever Phillips's sin had been, Diefenbaker eventually forgave him. The two became good friends in later years, to the day of Diefenbaker's death, which came shortly after he made his last television appearance on Phillips's CTV program.

The one chapter in Phillips's life of which I am ashamed, on my own account rather than his, came when he was named Washington correspondent for Southam News during the regime of Lyndon B. Johnson. Almost as soon as he took up his duties, Phillips got into the Vietnam story, and long before it became the fashion he was filing dispatches critical of the U.S. military effort and predicting its well-deserved failure.

His dispatches angered the Johnson White House and the State Department, and some of our newspaper publishers be-

"Tell the editor that me and the PM just had a little tiff."

Fights between reporters and politicians go back to biblical times. Here's how the Toronto *Telegram's* Al Beaton immortalized Bruce Phillips after John Diefenbaker ordered him off the prime ministerial campaign plane in the 1962 campaign. Courtesy Toronto *Sun*.

came uneasy about Phillips's objectivity. I kept expressing my trust in him, having seen the Vietnam war myself at first hand, but these were uneasy times. The State Department sent a press officer to the U.S. Embassy in Ottawa, whose job it was to blacken Phillips's name with his employers. The man's name was Ronald Moxness, and he toured the Southam papers, talking to anybody who would listen and preaching against Phillips's dispatches. He gave the assurance that the U.S. military effort in Vietnam was going well and would lead to a victory that would save freedom everywhere. Moxness administered his poison effectively. Some of the publishers believed him, and, as bad luck would have it, one of them engineered Phillips's recall from Washington.

Phillips, a gregarious man who became president of almost every club he ever joined, was prominent in the affairs of the National Press Club in Washington. He suggested the club hold a Canada Night one Saturday evening, with most of the organizational work being done by himself. The night took place and was a great success, but it wound up so late that Phillips decided to sleep in the Southam office in the National Press Building rather than go home. He curled up amid cartons of empty bottles from the party, and went to sleep on what subsequently became known as the Bruce Phillips Memorial Chesterfield.

Fred Auger, the publisher of the *Vancouver Province* and one of Phillips's most consistent critics, was making an unannounced visit to Washington at the time and elected to visit the Southam office early that Sunday morning, persuading the janitor to let him in. Entering the office, he came upon the sight of all the empties and of a sleeping figure on the couch, beneath a blanket of old newspapers. He lifted a sheet and called Phillips's name.

"Bruce," he cooed.

"Fuck off," said our hero.

"Bruce, it's Fred."

"Fuck off, Fred."

Curtain. The result was a motion for Phillips's recall, fought unsuccessfully by me, and that was an end of the critical dispatches about Vietnam until everybody got on that same theme and many prizes were won by the critics. Prime Minister

Pearson was one of the first statesmen to tell Lyndon Johnson he was a loser to his face, and got himself collared and cussed for pissing on the president's rug.

In our case, it was Phillips who got pissed on. Not long after his return to Ottawa he got the invitation to switch to television, and we lost our best, if not our most consistent, correspondent. As a glamour figure, Phillips was splendid in appearance. His voice was resonant, and, in content, he managed to keep his perspective better than most who do their stuff on camera.

There was one time, though, when I saw him throw his weight around, and that was in Espanola, Ontario, aboard the Stanfield campaign bus in the election of 1974. Espanola was in the heart of Algoma East, the most Grit riding in Canada, and Stanfield's visit was a token one, marked by a welcoming speech in which the local chairman boasted of Espanola's ethnic diversity, saying you could shoot a gun down the main street and hit a member of almost any ethnic group in the world. Stanfield thanked the chairman but said he had no intention of firing any bullets down the main street, "and besides, the fellow I'm gunning for isn't here."

When we boarded the bus that would take us to the plane in Sudbury, a man stuck his head in the door to say hello to Phillips and to ask if he would like some trout. At the mere mention of trout, Phillips, a lifelong angler, started to salivate. He said he would like some very much, so the man offered to bring him a dozen speckles from his freezer, which was just around the corner.

"Hold the bus," demanded Phillips.

No way, said the Tory wagonmaster, the bus must leave at once.

"This man," expostulated Phillips, "is bringing me trout. The bus must wait."

"The bus goes," said the wagonmaster.

"Hold this bus," fumed Phillips, "or else for the rest of the campaign we shoot nothing but crotch shots of your leader."

"Move the bus," said the wagonmaster.

"We're going to make Stanfield look like Quasimodo!" thundered Phillips, but the bus was moving, and there were no trout.

Next morning, under Phillips's hotel door at the Howard Johnson in Toronto, somebody thrust a smoked kipper. But Phillips remained inconsolable, and to this day mumbles about the lost trout.

Years later, he returned to Washington, all spiffed up as a counsellor at our Embassy, Her Majesty's press officer to the entire American nation. I rejoiced for him.

The First and Best Huckster

Political manipulation, incorporated into the modern antic arts of public relations, polling, and press agentry, goes back to Machiavelli, fondly cited in our era by his pupil Pierre Trudeau. It can be traced back beyond Machiavelli into ancient times, to Merlin and the backstage sages of Greece and Rome, who either fudged like the Oracle of Delphi, or were honoured when their advice was popular and put to death when it was not. That early custom of killing the messenger was illustrated by Cleopatra when she ordered swift dispatch of the courier who brought her the news of Antony's death, an event cited in today's Canada as often as Saul's conversion on the road to Damascus. Franklin Roosevelt had his Harry Hopkins, who was more crony than manipulator, though he had the president's ear in a way no other did, including Eleanor.

In our time, and our country, we have seen the art of manipulating politicians refined by the likes of Dalton Camp and Norman Atkins for the Tories, with assists from William Neville, Hugh Segal, and Allan Gregg — sometimes on the party payroll, sometimes on the payola list as consultants. The Liberals have had their Keith Davey, Jim Coutts, Martin Goldfarb, Tom Axworthy, and Bill Lee — sometime servants of Mike Pearson and subsequently Pierre Trudeau, and, in the case of Lee and Davey, John Turner to their regret, and his.

Most of the advice from these people was disastrous, but most of them prospered in fulfilment of the Peter Principle, Murphy's Law, and the early pronouncements of Professor C.

Northcote Parkinson. All have been glamourized by media, and accorded a respect never given to politicians by today's press corps. Yet few Canadians have heard of the man who pioneered the art in Canada, and whose success as a practitioner exceeds that of all the others, to this day.

When the Diefenbaker government was falling apart in 1963, and Defence Minister Douglas Harkness and Trade Minister George Hees had resigned, the Prime Minister was trembling so violently it was widely assumed he had Parkinson's disease. Our Bruce Phillips sang a song, to the tune of "Jesus Loves Me," that included this verse:

> There were rumours from George Hees
> I had Harkness's disease.
> You can take those rumours back,
> To that bastard, Old Mel Jack.

Old Mel who?

Jack had a lot to do with the public awareness of John Diefenbaker, propelling Dief to the leadership of the Tories and the prime ministership. And before that, he had struggled in the hopeless task of popularizing first Arthur Meighen, then John Bracken, and finally George Drew, in the dark Tory years when the Grits ruled the land under Mackenzie King and Louis St. Laurent.

Jack, though a scholar, had made no special study of how to succeed in politics. He did it all by instinct. The only poll at the time was the Gallup, and in his early years that U.S.-based organization scarcely paid attention to Canadian politics. He knew what was possible, he knew what would work, and he preferred to be behind the scenes rather than out front. He had a prodigious memory for names and faces, who was up and who was down, who could help and who could hurt. When he had the upper hand he knew how to inflict pain, as well as how to stroke.

Good as Mel Jack's political instincts were, they weren't as sharp as those of his wife, Blanche, who came from a rural Ontario background just as rugged as Jack's own in the Ottawa Valley. Some of his best thoughts were hers, and when he veered from her own thinking and told her to "be quiet," as he often did, she would refer to him as "Smelly Melly." It was a Beauty and the Beast relationship, because Blanche was the belle of Ottawa, though Jack complained that on the dance floor she had a Methodist foot. His own appearance was unmemorable, running to flesh and baldness, and you might not notice him unless you heard him talking fast or caught a glimpse of those flashing eyes, lit up either in anger or in mirth.

During the Depression Jack worked for the Great Lakes Paper Company, of which Arthur Meighen was the chairman and Earl Rowe the president. The air was thick with Tory politics, something Jack knew a bit about from his university years. One of his most vivid memories is of a by-election in the Ontario riding of East Hastings, when the Liberals under Mitchell Hepburn were in power.

"The issue was tax support for the separate schools," Jack remembers, "we were against it, and it was a Conservative sweep. Our big slogan had no words at all — people would meet one another and trace the sign of the cross in the dirt with the toe of their boot, then scratch it out. That meant you were against the separate school tax, and that's the way it was, and in parts of rural Ontario, still is."

Jack figured in two memorable by-elections during the Second World War, one a Tory loss, the other a win, featuring two men who stand tall in Canadian history, Arthur Meighen and General Andrew McNaughton.

Meighen was reputed to have been the finest orator ever heard in Canada, but his brief spells as prime minister in the 1920s didn't give him time to make his mark. He was languishing in the Senate when the Conservatives, smarting from their 1940 defeat at the hands of Mackenzie King, called him back to the leadership and he sought a seat in the Toronto area riding of North York. The Liberals laid back to give Meighen his entrée into the House of Commons, but the socialist CCF, ancestor party of the NDP, had other ideas and entered a candidate named Joseph Noseworthy against Meighen. Mel Jack remembers that what killed Meighen, and killed the Conservative Party in Quebec for decades after, was Meighen's statement that "when Britain is at war, Canada is at war." "There were socialist feelings in that by-election," says Jack, "and they've been around ever since. But what beat Meighen was the emerging wartime sentiment, 'let's be Canada.'"

That was the end of Meighen's leadership, but it was his idea to pass the Tory torch to an unlikely candidate, John Bracken, the Liberal-Progressive premier of Manitoba who had ruled that province for twenty-eight years. Bracken made it a condition of running that the party agree to add the word "Progressive" to its name, and it remains there to this day, as virtually the only reminder of Bracken's tenure. He won the leadership at the Winnipeg convention, one of the defeated candidates being the forty-five-year-old John Diefenbaker, who would have to wait another fifteen years for his chance.

Bracken came in triumph to Ottawa, and the rebirth of the Tory Party was widely trumpeted. Mel Jack was called to the boardroom of Great Lakes Paper, where Meighen and Rowe informed him he was to go to Ottawa to assist Bracken. His first job would be to accompany the new leader on a tour of the West. "They told me we were going to start a prairie fire out there and sweep every seat."

"So I came," Jack remembers, "and, Christ, we did the western tour. Start a prairie fire with that guy? There was no way. I suffered through some of the worst speeches I had ever heard in my life. When we got back east I went to see Meighen and said, look, there's no way I know how to make a prairie fire with this one. Meighen said I had to remember he was the only premier of any province or any country in the British Empire who was re-elected during the Depression. And by God, that was true. But what he used to do was pit rural Manitoba against Winnipeg, and it always worked, and on the strength of that we were supposed to win the West with a guy who wasn't even a Tory.

"I remember that one of our visits on that western tour was in Diefenbaker's riding, just outside Regina. Diefenbaker was there, still smarting from the convention, but very much the prairie lawyer on his home turf, welcoming the new leader. Bracken stepped up after being introduced by Dief and what he said was that he was going to give Canada a different kind of government, more along the Scandinavian system. He said 'no longer will Parliament and cabinet be run by lawyers — we've had too many lawyers. Farmers and businessmen will run the country, and if we need lawyers we can hire them.'

"There was Diefenbaker the lawyer sitting there, scowling, and that was the end of Bracken as far as Dief was concerned. It took seven years to get rid of him, because like many unsuccessful leaders he didn't want to believe he wasn't going anywhere."

I interrupted Jack to put in my own memory of Bracken, in the final year of his leadership, addressing a banquet meeting in the ballroom of the Château Laurier Hotel, his back against the big windows that face across the Ottawa River. Half way through Bracken's speech the audience came to the edge of their chairs, and then people started to stand up. Bracken thought he was getting the first standing ovation of his life. What he didn't know was that the Eddy Paper Mill woodpile in Hull had caught fire and the flames were leaping hundreds of feet in the air, the most spectacular blaze in the capital since the Parliament Buildings went up in 1916. Nobody heard what Bracken was saying, then or anytime.

The job was to persuade Bracken to leave. Says Jack: "Jim Macdonell handled it, and we thought we had it all arranged through a payment that was called reimbursement of expenses since leaving Manitoba. Well, he kept coming back with more details until finally it was agreed and Bracken spent the rest of his life as a gentleman farmer outside Ottawa, with two big farms he bought for a song. He was so happy he wanted me to buy one, too, and I was only an agent on the deal."

What about that other big by-election?

"Grey North," says Jack, with a smacking of his lips, "the dirtiest by-election ever fought, and there have been some dandies."

General Andrew McNaughton had been the commander of the First Canadian Army in Britain, the force he himself had described as "a dagger pointed at the heart of Berlin." The British, and in particular General Sir Bernard Montgomery, lacked confidence in McNaughton's generalship and insisted on his removal in favour of the more malleable General H. D. G. Crerar. McNaughton was relieved of his command and returned to Canada in rage and frustration, determined to enter politics and have his revenge on the hated Mackenzie King.

Mel Jack was secretary to Tory leader Bracken. "We were working on McNaughton, who was itching to come with us and run for Parliament in a by-election. The conscription crisis was mounting and the forces were hurting for reinforcements with all the casualties in Europe and Italy. Bracken had seen McNaughton this particular morning, then at lunch I asked Bracken how it stood and he said he was sure we were going to have McNaughton as a candidate.

"By God, about 4 o'clock that afternoon, John Connolley of British United Press came in and said he wondered if he could get some comment from Mr. Bracken about General McNaughton accepting the Liberal nomination in North Grey. I called Bracken and told him he could forget McNaughton, because King had just made him minister of defence. Bracken couldn't believe it. That's what made us so sore, and we threw everything we had into that by-election — every Tory speaker who could breathe, and Bracken himself in there four times.

"Our candidate was a reformed Liberal, Garfield Case, who was no mental giant, but could make copy. I don't think he gave too much respect to the laws of libel. McNaughton may have been the great military hero, but when Case got through talking about him he didn't look so good on a personal basis and you would have thought he was a parachute candidate for the Germans. It was quite successful, but it's good elections weren't regulated the way they are today or we'd all have been arrested."

Mel Jack had been aware of George Hees in Toronto before the war — "Gorgeous George" played for the Toronto Argonauts and won some notoriety as a gentleman boxer, taking part in bouts at Maple Leaf Gardens where, one night, a veteran pug grew weary of Hees's Fancy Dan tactics and nailed him with a right to the chin that put him out cold. Next boxing card, a Toronto sports writer advised the fans to "come early, and see Hees on his feet."

After George Drew became leader of the Conservative Party, Mel Jack continued under contract to work for the leader's office, advising MPs on speeches and press relations.

"About 70 per cent of my time was taken up with Diefenbaker," he says, "and the rest with Hees. They knew the value of publicity — those were the days when Diefenbaker was building up his reputation as a great civil rights man, though we didn't call it that. And Hees was the glamour boy, criss-crossing the country trying to put some steam in things. Drew eventually fired me as a suspected Diefenbaker supporter, which I was. Drew was always concerned about these other people getting the headlines — almost every leader is, unless he's very big."

Fired by the Tories, Mel Jack got a call from Walter Harris, who was then the Liberal minister of immigration in the St. Laurent cabinet, and was asked if he would do a survey on the utilization of manpower, especially the feasibility of using native workers, in the mines of northern Canada. The project made Jack a pioneer in the use of native labour, though his tactics might not be as acceptable now as they were then. The objective was to hire a native Indian work force for the newly opened Pickle Crow mine, and what Jack did was procure 100 Eaton's catalogues, published in colour, and visit the Indian wives, going through the catalogues with them, telling them "if you want this and this and this, get the old man to work, and he'll have credit, so you can place your orders."

"The guys went to work," chuckles Jack, "and the women went through all that colour stuff, and some of those Indians wound up putting their kids through university without a nickel of public support."

While working for the Grits, Jack was lending a helping hand on the side to Diefenbaker, and when Dief became Chief, he sent for his old friend. But so did Hees, and Jack says he chose Hees, "which was a wise move if you want to live. With Dief, one day if you had done something for him he was all pally wally and around your neck kissing you. The next day, you were fired."

With Hees, it was one triumph after another. Mel Jack was the genius of the piece, acknowledged by Hees himself who would arrive in the House of Commons, first as transport and then as trade minister, ready for any question, rising in his place with a laugh to brandish Jack's notes and say: "I just happen to have brought my music with me."

Transport was a huge department then, and the song we sang was "Hees' Got the Whole World in Hees' Hands." Airports were designed and built, airlines expanded, and Hees took the bows. As trade minister, he whipped the foreign trade service into a frenzy with the slogan "You can't do business sitting on your ass." Of Castro's Cuba, he said he had never encountered better businessmen.

Sometimes Diefenbaker applauded, sometimes he fumed. "One day," says Jack, "we were going west for the official opening of the Regina airport. That same day, Diefenbaker was speaking in his home town of Prince Albert, at a big dinner meeting to honour him as prime minister.

"At that time we had only two planes — and External Affairs Minister Howard Green had one and Dief had the other. So we flew commercial to Winnipeg, where we changed planes. We had an hour and a half in Winnipeg, and I phoned ahead to the press fellows there to give them Hees's text and have a talk, hoping they'd be scrounging around for copy. We did that and went on to open the airport, and next day Hees was front page across the country and Dief was about page 17. He hadn't handled it right, you see, he got his text out after he spoke, and what the hell, if you don't co-operate, you don't get it.

"Diefenbaker was livid and he told his people that was enough of being overshadowed — he was jealous of Hees to start with and I think he thought Hees was stupid, which in some ways maybe he was, but not politically. What George may have lacked, he had a way of getting out of other people."

Well, as Jack tells it, Diefenbaker had his chief aide Allister Grossart get hold of Mrs. Jack and tell her to sell her interest for a dollar so their jointly owned house could be put solely in Mel Jack's name. Why?

"Because Dief was going to appoint me to the Senate and you have to own property outright to be eligible. Well, Blanche phoned me all excited and I went right to see Hees and told him what a son of a bitch I thought he was, wanting to dump me and not having the guts to tell me.

"He didn't know bugger all about it, so I went and saw Dief the next morning and told him, thanks, but I'm not interested.

"Well Jeez, I never got such a lecture in my life. He said, 'I've got 300 applications for the Senate here on my desk.' I told him to give it to them all.

"He said he had never heard such impertinence. But he pulled back. That was going a hell of a long way to get at Hees, but that was his makeup."

There was another dust-up with Diefenbaker involving the People's Airline, originally called Trans-Canada Air Lines when it was set up in 1936 by the great C. D. Howe, who did more to industrialize and Americanize Canada than any other man.

"After twenty years," says Jack, "the airline had expanded, and opened service to Europe and various places in the United States. Gordon McGregor, who was then president, started getting all these recommendations about changing it to Air Canada. He came to Hees as transport minister and Hees said he thought it was a hell of a good idea, to go ahead, and that he would advise cabinet. But he didn't get around to it for a few days, and McGregor beat him to the punch by having a couple of the planes painted with the new name. When one of them landed in Winnipeg, the news got out.

"Well, Jesus! The anti-French feeling got to Dief, just as it did later over Gendarmerie Royale and the metric measure, and he blew up and ordered that the planes be painted back to Trans-Canada. The change didn't happen until the Grits were in office and put it through, so Hees never got the credit he deserved. A Liberal backbencher slipped it through as a private member's bill — his name was Jean Chrétien!"

Forsey rides again, as seen by cartoonist Ed Franklin. Courtesy *The Globe and Mail*.

Fun with Forsey

Colombo's Canadian Quotations is deficient in many ways, not the least of which in my jaundiced eyes is that in fifty years of journalism I penned at least 10 million words in assorted newspapers and books, not one of which caught Colombo's attention. Another glaring omission from the volume is any pungent quote from Eugene Forsey, that fountain of controlled exasperation who has tried, more in anger than in sorrow, to keep our national debates on the rails.

Forsey's academic qualifications are as awesome as his total recall of events going back to his birth in 1904, and as far beyond that as history has been recorded. His sense of humour is part Newfoundland, part Dickensian England, part H. L. Mencken, and mostly an unspoken decision on his part that, given the choice of laughing or crying, he would rather laugh — a marvellous cackle, ringing through his moustache, echoing through the corridors of Parliament or any downtown street on which you might encounter him and be swept into feverish discussion. I have met him on the ski trails in the Gatineau Hills, breaking in new equipment at age seventy, and I have rejoiced with him into his eighties and lamented his untimely forced retirement from the Senate, grateful that they kept a cubicle there for him as an unofficial office.

Before we sit down with him, here are some quotes culled from his last Senate speeches, to make up for Colombo's poor selection. *Over to Forsey*:

Nowadays for some people, everybody over thirty is absolutely ga-ga, utterly useless. They might as well be dead, perhaps better, simply cumbering the ground. If there are any honourable senators who do not like the way I am developing my argument, they are perfectly at liberty to leave. . . .

I have been horrified to discover, recently, that a great many of the contemporary political people and their officials have not the faintest notion who Edward Blake was. This nearly knocked me off my perch. . . .

Some people appear to think that flexibility is one of the cardinal virtues, that it is an absolute. These people, I think, might well propose that our national animal should be the jellyfish. On this matter of rigidity or flexibility, the value of these two attitudes depends on what you are being rigid or flexible about. . . .

Decentralize Canada? This gossamer, this shadowy, this cobweb central authority could also have a distinctive flag — 10 jackasses eating the leaves off one maple tree. . . .

The statement that Canada needs a new constitution and must have a new constitution and have it now is nonsense. It could be dangerous nonsense. You just give ground for every tub thumper, blatherskate, demagogue and cocksure jackass that happens to be loose in the country, and heaven knows there are enough of them of various kinds and descriptions. . . .

Parliamentary cabinet responsible government is the most delicate, the most flexible, the most efficient form of government the world has yet found, and the one most responsive to the public will; far, far ahead of anything the Americans, or for that matter any ruddy republic in the whole world, has ever discovered. . . .

Certainly the Crown is part of our British heritage. The whole basis of our constitutional law and our criminal law is part of our British heritage. We got these things from Great Britain — not from the Laurentian Shield, not from Paris, not from Rome, not from Budapest or Berlin or Vienna, we got them from our British heritage. This does not worry me in the least — it rolls off me like water off a duck's back. . . .

When people talk about the British North America Act being something that was imposed by the British government or the British Crown, they are talking through their hats. You have a British influence through those old scoundrels, those old rascals, the judicial committee of the Privy Council, messing up the work of the Fathers of Confederation....

Even in 1867, things like prisons, charitable or ele- emosynary institutions — a splendid word that, ele-emosynary, absolutely grand; Dr. Leacock used to roll it around his tongue with great unction — as well as a number of other matters which were of special interest and importance to the provinces, were left to them....

(To his Senate colleagues): You are stirring things up with an egg whisk....

Apparently I was misinformed, or I have tripped over my feet and fallen downstairs with the coal scuttle and the tea tray....

They say I advocated negotiation between Quebec and Ottawa on the issue of Quebec separation, prior to a Quebec referendum. That statement is wholly false. I made no statement even vaguely resembling anything like that. Everything that I said on the subject of negotiations made it perfectly clear to anyone who was not stone deaf, or lacking in the upper storey, what I was talking about. At no time have I ever, in public or in private, or even in thought, committed such a folly, such an idiocy, such a lunacy, as is reported in that statement....

June Callwood says the United Empire Loyalists consisted of people who hated democracy. This is highly misleading, highly contentious and factually erroneous. When I read this I went up in flames, and proceeded to write Mrs. Callwood a letter in which I drew attention in searing terms to this and other misstatements....

Some have the idea that judges are delegates of the government that appoints them. This, of course, is perfectly awful, nothing could be worse....

One of the advantages of having been a member of the CCF for so long as there was a CCF, is that anything over seven people qualified as a mass meeting....

I keep quoting St. Paul, "Let all things be done decently, and in order."

So much for Forsey's orations. Come sit a spell with him over a cup of tea and hear some of his tales, both of yore and of now.

What you get in a conversation with Eugene Forsey, when fun is afoot as it usually is, is Forsey the mimic, giving us stories in the tones of Newfoundland, or the Ottawa Valley, or the New Brunswick singsong. Forsey doing Arthur Meighen imitating Sir Robert Borden. Forsey as Diefenbaker, Forsey as Trudeau, Forsey in English with a Quebec accent, and in French with an English accent. It is a feast, and here are some helpings from our favourite octogenarian, indeed my favourite living Canadian.

Forsey: Meighen was a superb mimic of Borden — you could shut your eyes and you would have thought it was the old man in the room with you. His voice wasn't in the least like Borden's, but he would drop down several tones and it was absolutely perfect.

Borden once gave lunch to Clarence Jamieson, the member for Digby, at the Rideau Club during prohibition days. As Meighen told it, for Jamieson a meal wasn't a meal without a flagon of spirits, and as this repast wore on, Jamieson's mood got lower and lower. Finally, though, he felt a glimmer of hope — Borden leaned over to him and, in the confidential tone of prohibition times, whispered: "Jamieson! Jamieson! They have excellent . . . (and Jamieson started to salivate at the hidden pleasures about to be unveiled) . . . Deep Apple Pie!"

(Here I broke into Forsey's recollection to tell him about my own experience with Harry Southam, the proprietor of the Ottawa *Citizen*, whose eccentricities included temperance, along with Social Credit and faith healing and, eventually, socialism. Southam did not fraternize with his staff, but one Christmas he invited them to his Rockcliffe mansion and had them playing beanbag in his basement. Finally, he asked if anybody would like a beer, and the response was enthusiastic. To Southam, though, "beer" was ginger ale, and that's what we got.)

Back to Forsey: Another of Meighen's stories about Borden had to do with the Manitoba Boundary Extension Bill of 1912, and the proposal to build the Hudson Bay Railroad. There was a clause providing for a right-of-way five miles wide, and this got the Liberals very excited and in committee they went after the government very hard. Why on earth five miles? Where did that come from? Why not one mile? Or a hundred yards? The questioning was pressed by A. A. MacLean, Borden's colleague from Halifax, and finally Borden gave a reply that ended the matter abruptly, once and for all. Said Borden: "The subject appears to exercise a special fascination in the fertile mind of the senior member for Halifax. He, with his special pertinacity, keeps asking why five miles. The answer, Mr. Chairman, is that the matter was deliberated at length by Council, and five miles simply was deemed to be a convenient width. Deemed...to be...a con-ven-ient width."

Then there was the one about the proposed grant of $250,000 to Sir Arthur Currie, the supposed hero of the First World War. Meighen admitted that the Tory cabinet had agreed to make the cash grant to Currie. But when they took it to caucus, it was met with opposition from every quarter. Not one good word was said about it. Finally, Borden said he had heard sufficient — it seemed evident that the government's proposal did not command the assent of caucus: "I cannot see that any useful purpose would be served by prolonging the discussion. Indeed, had Sir Arthur himself been present and listened to what I've been listening to for the last half or three-quarters of an hour, I think he would tell us to take our $250,000 and stick it in our (long pause)...our...(pause)...EXCHEQUER!"

Humour is in short supply in Canadian labour circles, and Forsey is one of the few people inside the labour movement who could see the light side, even though he is the author of one of the weightiest tomes ever written about the workers' struggle. *Forsey*:

Funny stories about the Canadian Labour Congress are usually ones about Silby Barrett, the head of District 26 of the United Mine Workers in Cape Breton, and later on head of District 50, which took in chemical workers, hospital workers, and heaven knows what. Silby was a legend, an extremely able man, an excellent union leader, a first-class negotiator, and extraordinarily respected and even loved by the employers with whom he negotiated, because they could always depend on what he said. One of his trademark expressions was "leave us be honest," and he lived up to it. People knew if they reached a bargain with Silby, it would be lived up to, to the last letter.

Silby came from the east coast of Newfoundland, and he had a language all his own, and a sense of mathematics all his own, too. One time, he was down in Sarnia during the Ontario election of 1948, and he went to a meeting of his local union in the Dow Chemical plant. They were hearing from their local CCF candidate, a Mr. Humphrey, a school teacher, and as Silby told it, this Humphrey had been a powerful Liberal in his day but he was through with them now. "So," says Silby, "he tells the byes that the Liberal Party used to be a real reform party, but now they've gone all to pieces, and the CCF was picking up the true tradition of the old Grit party.

"Well, I could see dis wasn't gettin' nowhere wid de byes. I sez I'll handle this ting meself, so when he sits down I sez, Brother Chairman, can I say a few words, and he says sure, Brother Barrett.

"So I gets up and sez Mr. Humphrey here as given a whole fine history of the Liberal Party. Well, I h'aint much hinterested in de whole Liberal Party or the whole Tory Party eider. When I gets up to the pearly gates and meets St. Peter dere's lots of tings I'll have to confess, but not ever casting a Liberal nor a Tory vote. No, dat's one ting I never done.

"Now, den, I ain't a churchgoing man but I reads the good book sometimes like the rest of yez. And what does the good book say about the Liberals and the Tories? It sez it's easier for a camel to go trou de heye or a needle than 'tis for a rich man to get into the Kingdom of Heaven.

"TEEVES! Dats what the good book calls the Liberals and the Tories: TEEVES! An' den yez goes out and votes for 'em. You see me, ump-backed the way I am from workin', and I supposes yez tinks I wuz born dat way. No, I wasn't born dat way. Got dat way workin hard for a livin all my life with a lot of bastards on my back who made millionaries.

"When the CCF gets in den I'll be free. Den I'll straighten up. Well, when I finishes dat speech, the byes had some enthusiasm. So I finished by quoting the good book sayin' every man should sit under his own tree and eat the fruits thereof, but the Grits and Tories go one better, they'll divide up the fruit and eat 'em for yez!"

Silby Barrett's description of Newfoundland "hicebergs"

was: "Dey's hundreds of feet high an' yet tree turds of dem is under water!"

Forsey on Diefenbaker

The Old Chief was a constant critic of his successor as Tory leader, Bob Stanfield, and one day in the fall of 1968 something came up in the House on which Diefenbaker felt a statement was needed. "This is a subject," he told me, "on which Stanfield should be saying something. Instead of which, he is taking a two-week immersion course in Montreal, in FRENCH! Eugene, we Baptists know all about immersion. But we know enough not to stay under for two weeks!"

I sympathized with Diefenbaker's efforts to please Quebec, but he despaired of anything coming of it. Diefenbaker needed a lieutenant from Quebec, but he mistrusted every one of the fifty MPs he had from the province, and people kept telling him he had to look elsewhere, and the name that kept coming up was that of Marcel Faribault, of Montreal.

Diefenbaker came to call him "the ferry boat disaster," but when he was first recommended during the troubled days of 1962, Diefenbaker said "send him up."

"Mr. Diefenbaker," Faribault intoned, placing his hand on his heart, "it has always been my dearest wish to serve my country in Parliament."

"Well," said Dief, "when a man starts off like that with me, I have my suspicions. However, I said, that was fine. Where did he propose to run?"

"Sherbrooke." And then he said, "Mr. Diefenbaker, there is a minimum condition. I am not a rich man."

Diefenbaker said: "Just a minute, Mr. Faribault. You are worth between $750,000 and a million dollars."

"Where did you get that?" demanded Faribault.

"From a source which I think you would recognize as reliable."

"Well, be that as it may, I have five children, and I shall require from you a pledge for $500,000, payable in ten annual instalments."

Not one word, said Diefenbaker, about how long he would stay — one day, one week, one year.

"Mr. Faribault, if that's the minimum condition, good afternoon!"

"Then," Dief continued, "in 1965 the same great experts on Quebec said all my troubles would be over if I got Faribault, so again I said, send him up, and he came, and I offered him tea, and he said no. So I said: 'Now, Mr. Faribault, before we say anything else, that $500,000 nonsense is out.' And he said it was a complete misunderstanding. It was not a fixed sum, it was just this and that, this and that, this and that.

"To me," said Dief, "this made it ten thousand times worse, but I put it aside, and he said: 'Now, Mr. Diefenbaker, do you know who is the man in this country who knows more than any other man about external affairs?'

"Well, I thought Paul Martin thought he did, though Lester Pearson seems sometimes to kind of pull the rug out from under him. Faribault went on to say that he was the man who knew more about external affairs than any man in this country. So he said he would require a pledge that he would be secretary of state for external affairs.

"I said to him that nobody could give him that pledge. He would be promised a seat in the cabinet, but not a particular portfolio. That would make enemies of any one of the seven or eight other men who would want that portfolio.

"'Be that as it may,' said Faribault, 'that is my indispensible condition. And every policy decision in every other department must be shown to me before it goes into effect.' So I said to him that if that was the indispensible condition, good afternoon."

Stanfield eventually brought Faribault into the party, and it was a complete flop. He was president of the Trust Générale du Canada — when it came to anything about economics, he was way back in the eighteenth century, a hard-shell eighteenth-century Tory. But on anything that was theoretical, he was away in the stratosphere, and a Quebec nationalist to boot.

A lot of people thought Faribault was a great constitutional expert. He wasn't. And I'm not alone in saying so. Once he came to testify before the constitution committee, in 1971 or 1972, and he sent us 168 foolscap pages of his testimony. I went over the whole thing and he was full of contradictions. Elementary howlers. He had the British North America Act saying things that weren't there at all. I would have ploughed any first-year student saying those things.

Forsey's mention of howlers prompted me to ask him for the biggest ones he had encountered in his experience in public life. Forsey finds howlers in the laws of Canada, in the way those laws are interpreted, and the way Canadians misread their own history, or don't bother to read it at all. He tries to keep his indignation under control, but in his words, "when I see something that strikes me as nonsense, I promptly sit down at this thing and take a whack."

"This thing" is an ancient manual typewriter which was assigned to him when, as a senator, he was chairman of the Statutory Instruments Committee. He pinched it for his own use, and now that manual typewriters are classed as junk (along with most electrics) he feels no guilt about keeping it in the Senate office that is his by grace and favour of the government leader in the Senate, Duff Roblin.

Howlers in high places?

Forsey: The weirdest ones were those that accompanied the turnover from Pierre Trudeau to John Turner in 1984. They came in pairs.

First, the statement that it was unconstitutional to appoint a senator between the date of dissolution of Parliament and a general election.

I produced thirty-three cases in which it had been done without so much as a squeak of criticism from anybody. Mackenzie King did it fourteen times in one fell swoop. Both parties had done it, right back to 1874. Yet here in 1984 I was called by a Liberal member who said he had been told he would get a senatorship, but that somebody in Prime Minister John Turner's office had insisted on referring this to Gordon Osbaldeston, the clerk of the Privy Council, who said it was legal but would be politically inappropriate.

Well, I said, he's getting too big for his boots, that's not his business at all. That is for the Prime Minister to say, whether it's politically inappropriate or otherwise. The clerk had gone on to say that it would be constitutionally improper. I said, he's talking through his hat. Here's your list of cases. I remember when Meighen did it and King, who was always ready to yell "unconstitutional" even when Meighen brushed his teeth, didn't utter a word of criticism. Whatever officials have whatever opinions, it doesn't matter. What matters is that it's been done, by both parties, over and over and over again.

"But," he said, "the clerk maintains that now we have our new constitution, it's different."

I said no, there isn't one, it's only the old one with knobs on.

"But they say constitutional conventions are more important now."

And I said, this also is nonsense, the conventions are exactly what they were before, except for the provisions on amendments. The conventions are just what they were before, and just as important as they were before, no more and no less.

Second, the seventeen patronage appointments that Turner made, under that written agreement with Trudeau. Turner himself said he had got his advice from the clerk of the Privy Council, that he couldn't make the appointments before he dissolved Parliament because that would have cost the Liberals their majority. Osbaldeston told him that unless he had a clear majority in the House of Commons, he couldn't approach the Governor General to form a government.

Well, I said the clerk of the Privy Council has got the procedure hindside foremost. Nobody approaches the Governor General to form a government, the Governor General sends for somebody to form a government. This idea that you can't form a government without a majority of the members of Parliament in the House of Commons is nonsense. Lester Pearson did it, John Diefenbaker did it, Pierre Trudeau did it, Joe Clark did it, and Mackenzie King did it — formed governments without majorities. Talk about a howler!

Forsey drew a deep breath and shook his head. The trouble, much of the trouble, was that public servants had come to regard administrative convenience as a basic principle of the constitution, a distortion if ever there was one. That, and their tendency to fall back upon what they call "the dispensing power," a modern version of The King Can Do No Wrong.

Forsey cites chapter and verse from the proceedings of the

Statutory Instruments Committee, himself in the chair, and he reels off the facts with all the rage of a professor who has just flunked an entire senior class for bad spelling. *Forsey*:

In 1977 there came before us in the committee an instrument providing for the disposal of a considerable quantity of feed grain which belonged to the government. It was disposed of at a profit, but one of our duties was to see where the legal authority rested, to permit government action. In this case there was no legal basis whatsoever, and we discovered that the committee that made the sale had not been legally constituted until a year and eight days after the sale. We said, this is astounding, and most improper. And they said they had done nothing crooked. We said you didn't have the legal authority.

The officials were completely baffled, and considered it a mere eccentricity on our part, and it was one of many illustrations of officials, and ministers, under the illusion that administrative convenience is a basic principle of the constitution. They are wrong.

Here's another one:

There is a section of the Navigable Waters Act that says nobody shall dump noxious substances in any body of water. And a subsequent section says the cabinet can exempt any body of water from this provision. A regulation came through stating that Dennison Mines Limited was exempt, and we said it was ultra vires, beyond the powers given by the act. The act says you can exempt a body of water, and can stipulate that anybody can now dump this stuff in any body of water, but you cannot say Dennison Mines can, and everybody else cannot.

We said you can't use the dispensing power that way. And they asked what the dispensing power was, and we said it's a power which James II claimed for the Crown, to dispense with laws passed by Parliament, and which was made unlawful by the Bill of Rights of 1689.

They asked what Bill of Rights was that? They had looked in Diefenbaker's Bill of Rights and couldn't find it. Was it the American Bill of Rights?

No. Then what Bill of Rights was it?

The Bill of Rights which followed the Glorious Revolution of 1689.

What revolution was that?

I said, look — the dispensing power was one of the things that cost James II his throne. I learned that before I entered high school, and I know, because I can point to the exact book I got it from.

They had never heard of it. The next thing we knew, the lawyers from the Privy Council Office told us that the Bill of Rights of 1689 was no part of the law of Canada. At that, I went right straight up through the roof.

They said that if they couldn't dispense, they could exempt, and I told them to come off it. They wouldn't, and the only way we made any impression on them was to bring out, as a witness, Sir Robert Speed, Mr. Speaker's counsel at Westminster for thirty-two years. He was delighted to come, and we got him before the committee.

The Department of Justice had said a fig for our counsel, a fig for Forsey, Forsey isn't a lawyer at all, and he's past due anyway. But it was difficult to try the same game on Speed. So there were Department of Justice lawyers all around the room, with their tongues out and their ears flapping and their eyes popping. He said there could never be a regulation like that in Britain because it would be unlawful, made so by the Bill of Rights of 1689. We would just have to point that out and that would be the end of it.

And that was the end of it here, too.

They did try one other example of it on us.

There was a man named Jacques LeBlanc who had been involved in a murder. The people who were really most guilty were juveniles. They had got off relatively easily, but Jacques, being an adult, had got a much harsher sentence. The Parole Board decided this was hard luck for Jacques and they ought to do something about it. So they issued "special Parole Board Order Number One," letting off Jacques LeBlanc with a softer penalty.

We said they couldn't do it, and they asked why not. They said it was an exercise in the dispensing power. So we said they were empowered under the act to do certain things for "inmates," but not "an inmate." We said, "Look, you've got all sorts of means of dealing with Jacques LeBlanc. You can review his sentence, or pardon, or commute, but you can't do this. This is an exercise in the dispensing power which has been unlawful for more than two centuries."

They were indignant, and they took some convincing, but finally they got the idea.

Then we had a case with the Public Service Commission. They had appointed somebody by passing a special regulation. They could have done it by invoking another section of the act, but they hadn't. We asked for their legal authority, and they gave us a song and dance about what a wonderful man this was, how they could never have got him if they had used the normal procedure. We said yes, we weren't questioning his abilities — we just wanted to know where their legal authority was. They said they had had a legal adviser before, but they got rid of him because he was always raising points of law! We didn't succeed, though it was perfectly clear that the officials had no idea of law, or the place of law in society, or of the importance of law.

It still happens. Officials say actions are sensible, and useful, and helpful, and the best way to go, but it just won't do. If people ought to have power, people like fisheries inspectors, for instance, you must get amendments through Parliament.

Forsey closed our talk with more stories about Arthur Meighen, who, like Pearson and Diefenbaker, enjoyed jokes on himself.

In his early days in politics, he had driven out through a snowy winter night for a speech, and Mrs. Meighen went with him, along with Ted, who was a small boy. Driving home, Meighen asked Ted what part of the speech he had liked best, and the boy replied: "The part where the dog barked and had to be thrown out."

Meighen had been minister of the interior in the last days of Borden's cabinet, and in that capacity he had gone into a great deal of detail, insisting on knowing everything and making every decision. When he became prime minister, he gave the job of minister of the interior to Sir James Lougheed, Peter's grandfather.

Some time later he inquired how the department liked their new minister. He was told that on Lougheed's first morning he had called in all the senior officials and said: "You see that desk?"

There wasn't one thing on it — absolutely bare.

He said: "That's the way it's going to stay. I'm not going to run this department. I don't know a thing about it. You know how to run it. Go ahead. If you need help in the cabinet, or in the Senate, or on the hustings, come to me and I'll do what I can. Now clear out."

The message to Meighen was that Lougheed was "streets ahead of any minister we've ever had." And Meighen threw back his head and laughed and laughed and laughed.

One more Meighen story, this one involving Joe Clark's Uncle Hugh. Meighen and Clark were together listening to a paper on the life of William Lyon Mackenzie, Mackenzie King's revolutionary grandfather. The lecturer made the point that Mackenzie was long-winded, some of his speeches going on for hours, full of rambling disconnections.

Clark leaned over to Meighen and said: "Arthur! He must have inherited that from his grandson!"

"Did I tell you the story about Borden on Bennett?" asked Forsey.

Please do, said I.

Well, when Bennett was in the legislature of Alberta he was a maverick and a thorn in the flesh, not only to the local Alberta leader, who was Roly Michener's father, but also to Borden in Ottawa. Repercussions of what Bennett said in Alberta kept coming back and hitting Borden in the face. Then Bennett came to Ottawa as member for Calgary, in 1911, and some time in 1912 Meighen and Borden were walking up Elgin Street and they met Michener Senior.

Michener said: "Well, Borden, when R.B. was out with us, you used to complain that he caused you a great deal of trouble and you wanted to know why I couldn't exercise some degree of control over him. He's been here for a year now and I can't see you've exercised much control over him."

Borden said: "My God! Is it only a year? It seems like TEN!"

Our Crazy Crown

One of the funniest things about the way Canada is run is the monarchy, the font of all authority, the base of all our laws and loyalties, the keystone of all our oaths of allegiance and sworn secrecy. I have endured a lot of ridicule defending this ancient and honourable institution, some of it from the royals themselves, who don't give a damn who supports or opposes them in Canada.

They care about Canada when they are in Canada, and they care about Australia when they are in Australia, and the rest of the time what they care most about is Britain. They push hard for Britain around the world, especially when they are in their lost kingdom, the United States.

The obvious Britishness of the royal incumbents of our throne makes it hard for Canadian monarchists to explain their loyalties, which just goes to prove that the best loyalties, like the best loves, are the ones you don't have to explain. It's hard if you don't like Limeys, in which case you have a lot more problems than just the monarchy, for Limeys are everywhere in our society, always have been and always will be, resisting ethnic classification.

I like to think that my own loyalties to the Crown are based on logic. After all, the Crown in Canada meets at least three of the prime requirements of good government — it's cheap, it's honest, and it's absent. You couldn't invent it without risking certification for insanity, and you couldn't replace it if we ever let it go or, in the more likely event, that the Queen ever lets us go by abdicating and, with a single stroke of her pen, renders all our laws null and void. (The same is true of other complex, abstract, and unlikely institutions like the Roman or Jewish faiths, the Muslims, the Masons, the CFL, and the NHL.)

Besides, as Malcolm Muggeridge said, monarchy on the British pattern is more fun than all the other systems. There is more to laugh at, and more to cheer about, and less to hurt anybody or cause unpleasantness unless you happen to hate Corgis, or horses, or funny hats, or hereditary privilege. I enjoy all these things, from a safe distance.

It would be nice if we had a real crown instead of a pretend one — a crown, that is, made of gold and precious stones that the monarch could wear on her or his head whenever in Canada, on the Canadian expense account and rations.

For the royals, Canadian tours are a sort of penance they have to endure for all the boredom and torment Canadians have suffered at British hands through the centuries, though they might well feel that our men revenged themselves by taking it out on British women during the Canadian occupations of the island in the two world wars, while the British men were away. As Prince Philip once said to me, the royals don't do these tours for their health or their pleasure, and are quite willing to call the whole thing off if Canadians want them to.

But for Canadians, the tours are something special, as witness the crowds that turn out for the Queen Mother, the Queen herself, and for Charles and Diana, Prince Andrew, and sundry others of the ruling clan who pass through. That they do pass through is part of the beauty of it, in addition to keeping the costs down.

The Queen is something special, and always has been, right from her Lilibet days through her first visit to our shores and that marvellous photograph of her square dancing at Rideau Hall, at the start of her Canadian career. Now, when she comes among us, she sits and reigns, and we gape at her, and wish she would leave the British press back in London because of the foul things they write about us. They write foul things about her when she is in London, but let her come here and get folksy treatment from her Canadian subjects, and the British scribes get outraged. She never comments, being above the battle, though occasional human observations she makes at receptions for the press in Canada inevitably get into print, to the fake horror of the British correspondents. Elizabeth II is the most respected woman in the world, and she is ours. Well, partly ours. A piece of her, at a bargain price.

Quebec seems to want no part of her, and the French words to "God Save the Queen" are seldom if ever sung. Like the French translation of "Flanders Fields" carved into the Peace Tower, those words were written by bureaucrats to meet a requirement, rather than to answer any stirring of the heart.

I have suggested that Quebec become a republic within the confederation, the way republics exist within the Commonwealth. That would make the Crown a provincial rather than a federal institution, which is pretty much the way it has operated for the last twenty years anyway. Nobody takes any of this seriously, except me and the loonies of the Monarchist League of Canada, who are harmless. Nobody takes anything about the Crown seriously, which is part of the fun and gives us an edge over the republics and dictatorships where everybody takes everything about government very seriously indeed.

I argue that the Crown has been more useful to Canada than to Britain herself because it gives us a symbol of nationhood that is above politics. The Queen, of course, is not above British politics (ask any Irishman), but she is above Canadian politics, which qualifies her admirably as Head of State, something that no native Governor General could ever be. She understands our politics very well, as does the future King Charles, because they have visited Canada so often and had so many briefings about us, in addition to what they have observed at first hand when not attending those dreadful civic receptions we throw for them. In private, Elizabeth, Philip, Charles, and, doubtless, Diana, can mimic our politicians and have as good a laugh at our expense as we have at theirs, which is part of their Canadian identity.

You have to feel for the monarchy with your bones, and I'm not sure how the feelings are supposed to get in there. In some ways it's as complicated as the more unlikely religions, which have to be taught to the kids at an early age, or vanish. Nobody teaches our kids about the Crown when they are young, which is one reason the institution is failing and people like me get blinked at or tolerated as harmless eccentrics about to fade away. And yet our country continues to pass all its laws in the name of the absent Queen, and perpetuates her name and mythical authority in all our political acts, at home and abroad.

Our two countries, Britain and Canada, mean almost nothing to one another any more, and our interests coincide almost nowhere in the world. We know that in a crunch, as almost happened at Suez in the 1956 crisis when the interests of Britain and Canada were in collision, the Queen would listen to her British advisers over her Canadian ones, because they are the ones who pay the bills, including the rent. But we bumbled our way through that one and doubtless will do so again, conscious that nobody in Canada gives much of a damn about Britain, any more than anybody in Britain gives much of a damn about Canada.

We cling to the one tie, the tie of royalty, and we keep her face on our coinage and the cheaper banknotes, and a few of the more mundane postage stamps. She also adorns the Maple Leaf gold coins, though she's there only because she lends more prestige than a beaver. Her portrait hangs in the places where we do our official business, and few people glance at it, caring or otherwise.

New Canadians are said to be bothered by this, and foreigners are puzzled, some of them thinking it means Canada continues to be a colony of Britain. We tell them it is all a marvellous mystery, and they nod politely, the way we ourselves do when we visit foreign lands and have their customs and beliefs explained to us. Who would believe that New Hampshire is still governed by town meetings? Or that the U.S. judiciary is elected? And if people tell us our system stinks, we thank them for their interest and ask them to tell us more. Usually, we wind up thinking that however silly our system is, it's better than any of the rest.

The funniest thing of all, I suppose, is that we haven't had a Governor General since Georges Vanier who really believed in the monarchy in the Canadian context. I'm not sure Vanier did, for that matter. Roland Michener, Jules Léger, Ed Schreyer, and now Jeanne Sauvé filled the role of Queen's representative without displaying any vast enthusiasm for the Crown itself, and the same was true of prime ministers, from St. Laurent to Mulroney, with the exception of John Diefenbaker, whose origins were more Hun than Hon.

And there were times when I questioned even Diefenbaker's loyalty, during his squabbles with the Brits and his rage at the ceremonial opening of the St. Lawrence Seaway, when what he regarded as his rightful place at the side of President Dwight D. Eisenhower, in the reviewing stand, was taken by Her Majesty the Queen, with the Prime Minister of Canada relegated to the back benches. Diefenbaker was so sore he issued a temperance decree for the grand banquet marking the Seaway opening, a touch that must have astonished the Queen as much as it devastated the 2,000 guests, who set up bucket brigades from the nearby bars and bistros.

One of the problems the Canadian monarchist encounters is that there are so many crazies who feel strongly about the Crown. Indeed, some of the ones who belong to the Monarchist League feel strongly about royalty in all its forms and nationalities, and you have to keep reminding them that the only Crown you care about is the Canadian one, and not the Romanian, Bulgarian, or Russian, let alone the French.

A lot of the emotion has gone out of the issue in the last fifteen years, and I have long since stopped threatening to bop the next person who says anything against the Queen. The subject used to be good for a lot of incoming mail and telephone calls of support, usually from people with British accents, the very ones whose feelings matter least in trying to generate enthusiasm, or understanding, for the Crown in Canada. I have had women telephone me and sing "God Save the Queen" over the phone, encouraging me to join in. I no longer do, though I still think it is a splendid anthem. The words in English are more stirring, certainly, than the English words to "O Canada," which despite the launderings through the years still contain too much standing on guard. In fact, I find the English words to "O Canada" to be just about as stirring as the French words to "God Save the Queen," which may indicate the perils of trying to devise bilingual anthems.

One of the tests of an anthem is that each line of the chorus should be suitable as a book title. On this score, the English words to "God Save the Queen" pass with flying colours, especially the lines about sending her victorious, happy, and glorious. Even the American adaptation "My Country 'Tis of Thee" meets this requirement, topped by "Of Thee I Sing." You can get book titles out of "O Canada" — to wit, "Our Home and Native Land," "True Patriot Love," and even "In All Thy Sons Command." "With Glowing Hearts" is fine, and so is "We See Thee Rise" (a few "thee's" never hurt an anthem). Then comes "The True North Strong and Free" — not bad, even though Peter C. Newman stuck a "not" in there when he put it on one of his dust covers. Now comes the bad new line, "From Far and Wide." And a few bars later, "God Keep Our Land." Those lines were stuck in by a committee of bureaucrats, and any books with those titles would be remaindered on sight.

Sometimes anthems can get too complex, as in later verses of "God Save the Queen" which talk about confounding her enemies and frustrating their knavish tricks. Or they can get too long, as in the unexpurgated anthem written for the newly liberated Uruguay in the early 1800s by Giuseppe Verdi, which requires half an hour to perform and constitutes the first half of any concert at which it is played (they have a shorter one for everyday use). Sometimes they have a note that is too high to sing, as in the "Star Spangled Banner," all of whose lines have been used over and over again as book titles. And sometimes anthems are so stirring they don't really need words, as in the "Marseillaise," or the "Internationale," or "Boola Boola," the anthem of Indonesia, of which more later.

The best thing we could do with "O Canada" is for everybody to learn the French words and sing them together, though it would be helpful if English-speakers didn't bother to learn what the French words mean, or they might gag on that bit about the nation's arm being strong enough to carry the cross.

Quite apart from the religious overtones (God does keep cropping up in anthems), I have always suspected that when French-speakers sing about carrying the cross they are thinking about the burdens imposed on them by Anglos, hence the fervour they give to that line. We Anglos could return the feeling with equal enthusiasm, making a marvellous chorus.

Having said which, I close the case for the Crown by noting that the royals draw crowds when they come to Canada — friendly crowds, even enthusiastic ones, outside of Quebec, where they don't go anyway any more. And when public opinion is sampled, the vote always comes out heavily for keeping the Crown.

The One and Only Joey

After I described Joey Smallwood in 1972 as "the greatest rogue unhung," he stopped speaking to me and has held to that course steadfastly ever since. I am glad the falling-out did not come while Joey was still premier of Newfoundland — my offending words were used after he was overthrown, and when we were waiting for his successor, Frank Moores, to expose the supposed awfulness of the Smallwood years. Moores never did, of course, and now we are waiting for the revelations about Moores, just as future generations will wait for the truth about Brian Peckford, and so on into infinity as far as Newfoundland premiers are concerned, each one dreading to investigate the last.

Some of the best Joey stories have been told by himself. I've heard good ones from his own lips, as when he gave us a tour of his palatial farm residence outside St. John's and boasted that parts of the house and its furnishings were provided by contractors who had done work for the government. But they hadn't done it for him, he explained. They did it for the people of Newfoundland, who would have the place as part of their heritage after he was gone, so that made everything tickety-boo.

When Newfoundland entered Confederation and became part of Canada, Joey, as first premier, moved into what had been Canada House, the home of the recalled Canadian commissioner. Nobody in Ottawa had the nerve to ask him to leave and he stayed on for years, using the Canadian china, silver, and crystal, the stuff with the emblem. When he finally was persuaded to find other quarters, nobody ever found the dishes or the cutlery.

Frank Moores once told me that his biggest surprise when he took over from Joey wasn't anything he found in the files, because there were no files. It was a switchboard in the premier's office that enabled him to cut in on the telephone calls of any of his cabinet ministers, without their knowing. Moores had it taken out, but only after pondering its usefulness. Joey was a great eavesdropper — it was reported that, at the farm, he had the entire lane leading away from the house lined with hidden microphones, so he could hear what guests were saying about him after they departed.

I recall being in Newfoundland for one of Joey's landslide elections, and just as the polls were closing I crossed the lobby of the Newfoundland Hotel to go to the returning office to watch the results. Don Jamieson was on the television, doing the election anchor job, and he was giving a résumé of the election and its issues, without a note, and so I paused to watch the virtuoso in action, having once heard him refer to a local church dignitary as "His Arse, the Gracebishop." Jamieson's only rival as a TV free-wheeler was René Lévesque, and he gave us a ten-minute riding-by-riding summary of the campaign that was masterful. Just as he was winding up, there were noises off-camera and into view came Smallwood, pulling up a chair beside Jamieson. Now remember, not a single return had yet been reported.

Jamieson welcomed the premier and asked what he could do for him.

"I came," said Joey, "to tell you how I won this election."

"Pray proceed," said Jamieson, or words to that effect.

Joey was just getting into stride with his victory statement when the first return of the evening was shoved across Jamieson's desk. It showed Joey's candidate trailing his Tory rival by twenty votes to two. Joey didn't blink. He recognized the poll, which was in St. John's, and he named the streets and some of the Tory voters, and said he had spent time there that very morning driving people to the polls, but without much hope because he'd always had trouble there. He resumed his victory statement when a second result came in, from a poll in another part of the city. Again the Liberal trailed by a margin of ten to one, and Joey went into his description of that neighbourhood and its people, which was not flattering. He predicted the good news would be coming in shortly, which it did, and Joey wiped the floor with the Tories, as he did in every election but his last. Where else but in Newfoundland, I reflected, would a premier come on TV to explain his victory before a single vote was counted?

Another time the National Museum in Ottawa requested permission to come to Newfoundland to collect artifacts that would give the province its proper representation in the national collection. Joey agreed, but when all the artifacts were duly collected and crated for shipment to Ottawa, he seized them at dockside and opened his own museum in the old Province House, the building that housed the legislature before he persuaded American interests to build him a high-rise legislative building and lease it back to the people of Newfoundland.

While the nation's only skyscraper legislature was being built, he took a party of reporters on a tour of the premises, including the upper stories which consisted of bare steel girders. He wanted us to see the view from the cupola at the top, and by the time we reached it, most of us were airsick, clinging to the open scaffolding in a high wind. The cupola was built exactly to Joey's height, which meant that none of the rest of us could squeeze into it, so we hung from the girders while he showed us the view in every direction, not only the whole of St. John's and its wonderful harbour, but seven lakes, including one on the legislative grounds.

It was then he told us about his plan to put his fountain in the middle of the lake, the finest fountain to be found in the New World, imported from Europe where they know something about fountains. Joey had imported it, along with a bunch of heroic busts of Newfoundland's great ones, and had it installed beside the old Province House, but when he turned it on the old building shook and everybody for blocks around got drenched, so he had to turn it off and keep it that way until he found the new site. When it was installed in the lake he could turn it up to full volume, and did, and a wonderful sight it was.

We had Joey on TV in Ottawa at the time of the Newfoundland loggers' strike, after Diefenbaker had refused his request for RCMP reinforcements. Joey toured Canada whipping up support for his side of the argument, and drawing some of the biggest crowds ever gathered to hear a speaker, in city after city. On our CBC TV show, four of us were going to grill him, and Clark Davey of the *Globe and Mail* had the first question. Before he had finished asking, Joey cut in, saying the question reminded him of a story, and he held the camera in a twenty-five minute monologue that used up the entire time available for the program. There was a live hockey game coming on after us, so finally I interrupted Joey's flow and said I was sorry, but we were out of time. Joey said he was sorry, too, because he had a lot more to say. The network was subsequently deluged with telephone calls and telegrams denouncing me and my press colleagues for being rude to that nice Mr. Smallwood and not letting him finish.

For a while there, we had Joey in Newfoundland, Wacky Bennett in British Columbia, Diefenbaker in Ottawa, Maurice Duplessis in Quebec, and Tommy Douglas in Saskatchewan — there may have been more exciting times in Canadian politics but I can't think when they were. Funny times, and crazy, and good.

Sir Wilfrid Among the Tories

Some of the miscreants in the following story are still alive, and if they are asked about it, they will deny all. But I have it on the word of one of the participants that it is true.

On a plinth in the Albany Club in Toronto, the Tory holy-of-holies, stands a bust of Sir John A. Macdonald, but it isn't the one that was there when the club was founded. One night, almost fifty years ago, some members of the club had been roistering in an upstairs room, and upon descending the stairs after midnight, one of them noticed that the bust of Sir John was dirty. So they picked it up and took it into a downstairs washroom and put it under the tap, and went back upstairs for another round. When they returned to get the bust they discovered to their chagrin that, rather than being marble as they had thought, it was plaster-of-Paris. And it had melted half away, little remaining but the wire frame and some gobs of goo.

Mitchell Hepburn was in power in Ontario at the time, and he was a Grit, but one of the culprits said he was a friend of the premier and would call him at his suite in the King Edward Hotel to see if he would agree to let them have a replacement bust of Sir John. So they roused Premier Hepburn out of bed and, being a drinking man himself, he caught the spirit of the occasion and agreed, though it was now 2 A.M., to phone the legislative building at Queen's Park and arrange for the visitors to be granted admission and permission to borrow a bust of Sir John A.

The mission was accomplished without a hitch, and the lads

returned in triumph with the statue, which was placed on the vacant plinth just as dawn was breaking. They then lugged what was left of the old bust away for repairs and, within three months, the original of Sir John was back, good as new, and was put back in place, while the borrowed bust was returned to Queen's Park.

What no member of the Albany Club had noticed was that the bust that stood in their midst during all those weeks and months wasn't Sir John at all. The statue purloined with Hepburn's permission was that of the nation's leading Grit — Sir Wilfrid Laurier!

The Day They Shot John Diefenbaker

I'll never forget the day they shot John Diefenbaker. So I was told. It was November 22, 1963, and I was in Djakarta, the capital of Indonesia, attending the Games of the Newly Emerging Forces, or GANEFO, as Indonesian dictator Sukarno called his Third World rival for the Olympics.

I had seen Sukarno strut his stuff in the giant stadium the Japanese had built for him, and I had marvelled at how the Indonesian national anthem sounded like the Yale song "Boola Boola." And the okay had come through for an interview with the mighty Bung, as he was called, at his country palace in the mountains, at Bokor.

I was picked up in the morning by a carload of Sukarno flunkies and we were headed out of Djakarta when one of them said to me that my leader had been shot, that morning.

"My leader?" I asked, incredulously.

"Your head of government," the official nodded.

"Lester Pearson has been shot? Who would want to shoot him?"

"No," came the reply, "I can't remember his name, but not Pearson."

"Well," I said, "Pearson is prime minister in Canada."

"Some other name," said the official.

I groped, trying to think which Canadian leader anybody would want to shoot.

"John Diefenbaker?" I ventured.

The official's eyes brightened.

"That sounds like it," he said. "Shot!"

"Is he dead?" I asked, trembling with sudden affection for the Old Chief.

"They're not sure," said the official. "The report just said badly wounded."

We drove for two hours and a half, in the course of which I mourned for Diefenbaker and recalled the many good and bad times we had had together, and how his arms waved and his wattles jiggled and his hair flew when he was in full cry. It was hard to imagine that vibrant voice stilled, to be heard no more.

I finished the trip in silence and we trooped into the vast estancia maintained by Sukarno, where I was informed that the interview would not take place but that I was welcome to attend a gathering of Sukarno's cabinet, already in progress.

"What happened to the interview?" I asked.

"It is because of the death of President Kennedy," came the reply.

"President Kennedy?"

"Shot in Dallas this morning and he's dead. Bung Karno is trying to decide whether to go to Washington for the funeral."

I had to switch my thoughts from Diefenbaker to Kennedy, and the massive impact of the event hit me, heightened by the fact that there seemed more merriment than mourning in the Sukarno entourage. The place was full of beautiful women, one of them Sukarno's fourth wife, and the rest wives or companions of the ministers. Sukarno moved among them, patting the women and wielding a pair of scissors, with which he proceeded to cut off the neckties of various cabinet ministers, who joined in the general mirth. I felt that if he tried to cut mine off I would retaliate.

I needed someone to cry with, but there was nobody. The presidential decision was not to go to Washington for the funeral, and business, such as it was, went on as usual except for my interview, which I no longer wanted anyway. After the long drive back to the capital I found my way to the United States Embassy, where the flags were at half staff and the windows draped in black. I went in and had my cry, tempered only by the strange thought, exclusive to me on that day, that at least John Diefenbaker was still alive.

I have one more tale about Sukarno, told to me years later by the third secretary of the Indonesian Embassy in Ottawa, himself a veteran of the Sukarno regime. This man had been stationed at the Indonesian Embassy in Lisbon when it was announced that Sukarno would be making a state visit to Portugal. Amid the fuss and feathers of preparation there came a coded cable from Djakarta to the effect that women should be provided for Sukarno's famous diversions, and the third secretary was instructed to make the arrangements. Being a quiet-living man himself, he did not know where to turn, and finally confessed his predicament, on oath of secrecy, to a friend who was a junior officer in the Portuguese foreign office. The friend pondered for a while and came up with a solution. "What you must do," he said, "is find a nice whorehouse and book the whole place for the duration of your president's visit. Then you'll have women galore for whatever his whims dictate."

The Indonesian diplomat thanked him, and the two of them went off together to find a suitable house and make the arrangements. The madame named a price for a one-week, night-and-day reservation of the house and all its inmates, and the money was provided without further questions by the Indonesian ambassador, who said with a shudder that he wanted to hear no more about it.

On the eve of Sukarno's visit, word came through that the trip was cancelled. Sukarno would not be coming after all. The Indonesian diplomat and his Portuguese friend went around to notify the madame and get the money back. Nothing doing, said the madame. A deal was a deal. No refunds. "What do we do now?" the Indonesian diplomat asked his Portuguese counterpart. "There is only one course of action," said the Portuguese, smiling. "We move into this whorehouse and stay for a week!" Which they did.

Sukarno made his European visit eventually, but there was no need for providing female companionship because he was travelling with Gina Lollabrigida, leading people to say that with all his faults, the old Bung always had a good eye on him.

Last of the Big Bagmen

Bagmen and bagladies have at least one thing in common. They forage. Bagladies forage in city alleys, picking over garbage. Bagmen forage in corporate offices and boardrooms for money, in the form of political contributions. Bagladies never get rich, or appointed to the Senate. Bagmen, if they aren't rich to begin with, seem to get that way, and the Senate is full of them. They don't get to keep any of the money they collect but they seem to build up contacts, and just knowing where the money is helps them to get some. The Senate appointment is merely the capper, and sometimes it comes early, sometimes late.

For Finlay MacDonald it came late, and it almost didn't come at all, since so many Tories were in line by the time the party got into office in 1984. Brian Mulroney's ultimate joke on Finlay was to let him hear about his appointment from a woman in the prime minister's press office, who phoned Finlay to ask when his birthday was.

"Why?" asked MacDonald.

"For this press release we're putting out this afternoon."

Long pause. "What's it about?"

"Your appointment."

"My appointment to what?"

"It says the prime minister is pleased to announce the appointment to the Senate...." At this point Finlay stopped hearing and started cheering, to the surprise of author Ron Graham, who was in MacDonald's office at the time.

Then, in a husky voice, MacDonald croaked down the phone: "You wouldn't shit me, would you? What did you say your name was?"

"Valenti."

"Do I know you?"

"Not until after I've consulted my crystal ball"

Finlay MacDonald thought about running for the Tory leadership in Nova Scotia in 1971. Halifax *Herald* cartoonist Bob Chambers depicts MacDonald seeking guidance in the gleaming pate of his pal, Dalton Camp. The message was "Don't go, Fin." Courtesy of The Halifax Herald Limited.

"No, senator."

"Say it again."

"Senator."

"Sweetheart!"

And MacDonald hung up and said to Graham: "If that wasn't another dirty trick from our mimicry department, I think I've just been appointed to the Senate."

So they both had a drink, and it was true, and later that day Mulroney phoned MacDonald and talked of many things, and at the end of the conversation the prime minister said, "Oh, yes, there was one other small thing, I approved your appointment to the Senate this afternoon: Will you take it?" "It's took," answered MacDonald, and they both laughed.

The story of how MacDonald wound up with the finest and most historic office in the East Block takes longer to tell, and involves the senator outwitting what he now calls "those nerds in the PMO." It was in that office that we talked and he told me what it means to be a party fundraiser, an activity that he transformed from a grubby business to a fine art.

Finlay, unlike most of his kind, actually ran for Parliament and got defeated, in 1963, when Halifax was a twin riding and the winners for the Liberals were a couple of unknowns named Regan and Lloyd. For Gerald Regan it was the start of a long and illustrious career — and listening to the returns that night over his own TV station, MacDonald heard himself described as the candidate "who shook the hands of 40 per cent of the voters, and the confidence of the rest."

That made Finlay a backroom boy for the rest of his political life, and he played the role with smoothness and suavity and, Lord, how the money rolled in. When he laid down his burdens at last, and put the olive wreath on his brow, the Progressive Conservative Party was the best-heeled political organization in Canada, if not in the free world. How did it happen?

I note that MacDonald says business people stay out of politics because they haven't got the guts to come in, to run, to campaign, to take the heat if they win. And then I suggest that money keeps a lot of people out — it's just too hard to stay out of debt, win or lose.

MacDonald: No, I don't think money is a big problem for a person running for office. The public assistance they get helps a lot. People put themselves more in debt running for an office inside the party — those $15,000 or $20,000 campaigns to become treasurer or secretary or a vice-president. God knows, both of us have been to fundraisers to try to clear the debts of the Don Johnstons and Jack Horners who run for leadership, where there's no limit on spending.

But that's changing. The biggest changes I helped to make, though, were in raising funds for the PC Party itself. Remember that in 1972, when I was campaign chairman, all of our money was collected from 1200 corporations. In the election of 1984 there were over 100,000 contributors, of which only a quarter were corporations. Now, that's a healthy development, utilizing modern methods right down to the constituency level.

When I became the chairman of the PC Canada Fund I went to our consultants and said there were going to be a few changes made. First of all, the letters we were sending out were offensive. They were five pages, when one would suffice. And they said, with all due respect, they were in the business as professional fundraisers for the Republican Party in the United States, and they were our consultants. Did they mean to say, I inquired, that a five-page letter makes more money than a four-page letter? And they said I was getting it. Five pages did better than four. Four did better than three. And three better than two. And with one page, we'd go broke.

So I agreed to a test on our next mailing, an elephant hunt as we called it, where we rent lists wherever we can get them and send out a million letters with all sorts of distortions and duplications, including columnists getting copies and letters going out to Dear Public Library, or Dear Parts Department of Atlantic Chev-Olds. We split the lists in two, and they wrote their letter, five pages, beginning "Dear Friend of the Conservative Party, Trudeau sucks! We know that you know that the forces of evil" etc., etc., for five pages of invective. They told me that this kind of stuff would spark, in 2 or 3 per cent of the people, that desire to respond, and thereby put themselves on our tape forever as contributors to the Conservative Party. My letter, which I worked on for weeks, was one page, and it was masterful, and it didn't even come near to recovering the stamp money needed to send it out. That made me an instant believer, however much distaste I might have had for signing the five-pagers.

Now, it has to be remembered that when you're in opposition you have an enormous opportunity with direct mail. The civil liberties people in the United States were going broke until the Reagan administration came in. Then they had a target, and now they're rolling in dough, with Reagan as their Force of Darkness. In opposition, we heaped calumny on Trudeau in particular and the government in general. The same consultants were acting for our party in Ontario, where we were in power, and they were having trouble with letters saying "Dear Fellow Conservative, Our distinguished statesman Bill Davis needs your help," and back would come letters telling them to stuff themselves. In our current federal campaigns, if you want obscenities, all you have to do is read the return mail from letters which now have to defend the government, saying that the good work of Mr. Mulroney must be continued and for this purpose more money is needed — say, fifty bucks.

People claim we have to reduce corporate giving, so the party won't be the party of Big Business. I ask for proof of influence of big corporate givers and nobody has any. The big donors are the most naïve people in the world; all they want is an opportunity to get their point of view across, or get to face a minister. All the names are listed. Look at the chartered accountants — we turned the screws on the big firms and suggested they give fifty thou apiece and they almost shat their pants. But they gave, and we got into power, and look what happened in the hearings on the western banks? The big accounting firms got scorched at the hands of our MPs on the committees. With friends like us, the accountants don't need enemies.

Another thing — when a party's in power and it gets in trouble, the corporate givers run like rats off a sinking ship; it's the little donors who are more likely to stay with you. The corporates, of course, give without conviction to both parties — the small donors put their hearts into it.

As for individual candidates, sure it's odd to limit them to a third of what people spend in civic elections across the country to get elected mayor. But it all evens out as long as the rules apply to everybody and one candidate can't spend $200,000 — as Dalton Camp once did in Don Valley and lost, to Dief's delight.

Sure it's nice to have money, but I'm reminded of the boxing card in Madison Square Garden where a Catholic priest was sitting at ringside, and a Mexican kid got into the ring and made the sign of the cross. A guy beside the Father said he wasn't a Catholic, but did that sign of the cross help? "It will," said the Father, "if he keeps his guard up and can punch."

The field is littered with all the heavily financed candidates who didn't make it — Roy Thomson, Pierre Juneau, Maurice Strong, John Evans, John Bassett.

Bassett! There was a guy with all the money in the world,

the *Toronto Telegram*, his promotion of ethnic causes, and big with the Jews. He ran in Spadina and got himself royally screwed. I saw him soon after and asked him what happened, and typical Bassett: "What happened, for Christ's sake, Finner! I mean, Jesus Christ. Ya come back a war hero for Christ's sake and then you become a handsome, talented, rich, crusading newspaper publisher. Look, I mean, they don't go for that kind of bullshit any more!"

The business of fund-raising is like a disease with some party people. They're money-raising junkies. They all owe one another. I had four fund-raising letters for Bill Jarvis's campaign for party president, and I kept saying the guy was in by acclamation. Yet Terry Yates wrote me, and Bill McAleer, Fred Dickson, and Pierre Fortier, and the solicitations kept coming. So somebody made up an accounting and read it at a dinner we had, showing expenditures of $1853.61 for travel, $850 for hotels, $4900 for stationery and printing, $4600 for signs and bunting, total with miscellaneous, $21,000. Revenue, $377,900. Three cheers for Il Presidente!

You know, the people that God loves most, he has given a sense of the incongruous, the cosmic joke. Generally speaking, these are people who find it difficult to be cruel or to be character assassins. Like Bob Stanfield — a real gent who got the joke.

Taras Shevchenko
and the Arsole Story

Mention Stanfield, and I think of Grogan. There is a legend, or
perhaps no more than a suspicion, that William Grogan is a
descendant of mad King Ludwig of Bavaria, the man who built
all those castles and bankrolled the works of Wagner, and kept
Lola Montez in the style to which she became accustomed.

Grogan has the royal upper lip and a regal carriage when he
is swaggering, especially onstage, where he is at his best.
Friends of Grogan hold to the view that, had he chosen a career
on the boards instead of in the boardrooms, his name would be
a household word, as it is in the circle of those who know him
and marvel at his musical and Thespian talents. When we were
doing the Mouseketeer number quoted earlier in this volume,
Grogan, with no more props than a set of ears and short pants,
actually turned into a mouse onstage.

I have seen him turn into George Formby, Ed Broadbent,
Don Jamieson, David Lewis, Brian Mulroney, and Allan Mac-
Eachen. He can do opera, he can do slapstick, he can go into a
snit and tell everybody to go to hell — and mean it. Grogan is
one of those men who can make you put up with the bad times,
for the good times.

I was telling Grogan about travelling in the Soviet Union
with Trudeau in 1971, when, as dean of the visiting press corps,
I had to make some speeches. I reached my peak in Kiev, where
I was able to tell our hosts about the high regard Canadians
have for their native son, the great poet Taras Shevchenko. We
toured the Shevchenko museum, and the Shevchenko home,
and we visited the Shevchenko monument, and each time I told
about the Shevchenko statue on the grounds of the legislature in

Bill Grogan was Robert Stanfield's court jester and often had to make bad news sound good. This time it was: "Now the GOOD news — there's no election!" Courtesy *The Ottawa Citizen*.

Winnipeg, dedicated by our own great prime minister, John Diefenbaker. And it was that same Diefenbaker who arranged, each year he was in power, for the business of our House of Commons to be interrupted on Shevchenko's birthday, when members of all parties would pay tribute to the bard.

In vain did the resident representative of the Canadian Communist Party whisper to me that I was praising Shevchenko for all the wrong reasons — that the real Canadian monument to him was in a Communist cellar in Toronto, and that the Winnipeg one was erected by Ukrainian fascists, who had claimed the poet for their own. Similarly, the praises for Shevchenko in our Parliament came from Fascist lips. But I persisted, and if our hosts felt I had got it wrong, they didn't say anything, at least not in any language I could understand.

Grogan laughed, and recalled the day Diefenbaker dedicated the Shevchenko statue, which coincided with the advent of portable tape machines at Radio Station CKY, where Grogan was one of the top on-air personalities of the time. The new Ampex tape machine was sent off to the dedication ceremony, and when the tape came back to the station it was Grogan's job to slice out a brief clip for the evening newscast. He listened to the speech with growing unease, as Diefenbaker quoted at length from the translated works of Shevchenko, without saying anything that would contain a wallop in ten seconds.

Then Grogan heard it. Diefenbaker worked himself up into a fever pitch about the brotherhood of man, as proclaimed by the poet, and he proclaimed, in his most stentorian tones, that "Our souls are tied together!" Long pause, for effect. Then: "ALL our souls are tied together!"

So, says Grogan, "I put it on a little piece of tape and made it part of the newscast package, with an intro setting the scene. Well, we ran this clip on the noon news, a couple of times in the afternoon, on the major news package at supper time, and later in the evening. And it got some more play next day, which was Sunday, by which time it was ready for the waste bin, except that the phones began to ring after the first newscast without the clip on it.

"A typical call would ask where was the story about Dief and the arsoles — there were still people who hadn't heard it, and they were gathering around their sets. So we had to take it back out of the ash can and run it more times, and the requests went on and on. Play arsoles. It got more requests than the top ten songs. Monday, we ran it five times, and we were running promos on the air saying the excerpt from Mr. Diefenbaker's speech would be heard on the next newscast, for those who had phoned in to demand it. It went on through Tuesday and, finally, other news was piling up and the program director, Jack Stewart, said get that damn thing off the air, he never wanted to hear it again. So we took it off, but I still have the tape to this day."

Grogan went on to become a policy adviser and court jester to Robert Stanfield, when Stanfield replaced Diefenbaker as Conservative leader. It was Grogan, as much as anybody, who was responsible for the fact that virtually everybody in the Stanfield entourage came to talk like Stanfield, with those long pauses that Stanfield insisted were part of his comic timing.

Grogan recalls a time, in the fall of 1970, when Stanfield was visiting Toronto and the musical *Hair* was playing at the O'Keefe Centre. Stanfield spent the afternoon walking about downtown Toronto staging a series of photo opportunities, though that expression had not yet been invented. That night, Stanfield went off to see *Hair*, and next morning he travelled to Hamilton to keep a promised date with TV reporter Geoff Scott at CHCH-TV, for an in-studio interview.

Grogan: When we got to the studio, Stanfield took his place while they got the set arranged, the lighting fixed, the make-up in place, and Geoff, to make conversation, asked Stanfield how he had enjoyed *Hair*. Stanfield chortled and said he had quite enjoyed it, quite enjoyed most of it, though he thought parts of it were a little forced — a little extreme, a couple of places.

All through this, Stanfield's voice was booming into the control room for the sound checks, and speakers were carrying it all through the station. Everybody seemed excited to see and hear Bob Stanfield right there in the flesh, and his voice was booming, and Scott kept pressing to find out what there was in *Hair* that Stanfield had found forced.

So Stanfield described one of the scenes where a fella comes out one side of the stage and says "fuck!" And then another guy appears on the other side of the stage, and he says back at him, "fuck!" And the two of them just stand there for a couple of minutes yelling "fuck! fuck! fuck! fuck!" And by this time the sound guy in the station had turned the pots up full blast and everybody in the place, male and female, heard the great voice of Stanfield hollering "fuck!" I wouldn't say Stanfield had been offended by the lines in the play, just bored. But it was quite a moment at CHCH, and nobody there ever thought after that that Bob Stanfield was a stick-in-the-mud, and Geoff Scott went on to become the member for Hamilton East.

As for Stanfield, he became known to insiders as the best stand-up comic ever to lead a political party in Canada, though this was kept a secret from the voting public. A lot of his best lines were written by Grogan, but the timing was Stanfield's, and sometimes the lines were, too — witness his comeback when an unfaithful colleague, James Gillies, announced his intention of throwing his hat in the ring for the Tory leadership and Stanfield said: "I hope it's not one of your good hats."

The Funnybone Man

Few people knew that one of the most boring men in Canadian politics could also be the funniest. Robert Stanfield chose to suppress his funnybone in public and thus never did get to be prime minister. Had he done so, chances are he would have become known as the dullest prime minister ever, and the nation would have dozed off through the turn of the century which, considering the way things have gone, might have been just as well.

Those who knew Stanfield were well aware of his sense of humour, though the public remained largely in the dark about it and regarded him, as the cartoonists and mimics did, as a sort of Boris Karloff in his underwear. Stanfield was a constant victim of Murphy's Law, a problem that confronts all federal leaders of the Progressive Conservative Party. Though he was from Nova Scotia, he despised the sound of the bagpipes and, once elected leader, asked that there be no "piping in" when he entered halls across the country. Result: there was no hall unpiped, and they skirled him until his bony head spun.

When he retired, full of years if not of honours, he was the first and only politician in the country without an enemy. My own contribution to his farewell roast in Halifax was to declare I wasn't going to say anything to Stanfield's face I hadn't said a hundred times behind his back. Here are some quotes of his comebacks at that affair, and some other gatherings where he was letting his bright side show. *Over to Stanfield*:

'You can't roast a wet blanket.

The cameras here don't bother me, or the lights. I've been on the CBC before . . . Once or twice even during the last election!

You won't have Bob Stanfield's football to kick around any more.

Charlie Farquharson has been out of the country so long he thinks the Speech from the Throne is only delivered when the paper runs out.

Who ever heard of Lynch before I drew national attention to him by sharing the spotlight in starring roles with the National Ballet in Ottawa, in the *Nutcracker Suite*? Before that, he was just wandering around the country looking for opportunities to play "O Canada" on his mouth organ. He is unique among Canadian journalists. He's the only columnist I know who's made a good thing out of being wrong all the time.

Following the 1974 election I was sitting in Halifax, pondering my political future, when Judy LaMarsh wrote a column saying some very kind things about me. I knew then that my fate was sealed, that I was finished. Have you ever been embraced by Judy LaMarsh?

Remember what C. D. Howe once said, that he was as busy as a happy hooker working two beds?

I remember after the 1972 election, sitting there waiting for that telephone call from the Governor General. My friends, whatever the telephone company may say, that's not the next-best thing to being there!

And here he is, at the Variety Club in Toronto, on May 27, 1971:

In two countries, the United States and the Soviet Union, I have found it hard to explain what it means to be the Leader of the Loyal Opposition.

• Confusion is understandable in the case of the Soviet Union, where I tell them that in our country the head of the government at least knows who the leader of the opposition is, and can keep tabs on him. In Russia, once the government knows who the leader of the opposition is, it may be too late to do anything about it.

There is bewilderment in the United States too. Their papers call me Canada's Number Two politician. That means I must be trying harder. Other politicians try hard, too, and can be very trying, like the minister of finance. Now, that is a thankless and a lonely job, particularly when you're bad at it, totally dedicated to spreading poverty evenly across the country.

(I'm sorry I'm too fast for you fellas.)

The Liberals take their text from Masters and Johnson — "How to really enjoy several different positions."

I knew Trudeau would never marry Barbra Streisand, because I had heard him say so many times that "the States has no place in the bedroom of the nation."

They say Trudeau has no respect for the past. It is obvious he has a great feeling for our history as a nation of pioneers who slaved and starved to maintain this country when Canada was a wilderness. If he didn't have this kind of affection for us, why would he be trying so hard today to restore those conditions?

Trudeau says the Liberal Party is the kind of organization that you can join freely, and leave freely. I guess it's only between joining and leaving that there's no freedom at all.

The only minister that's still firmly with Trudeau is Billy Graham. There's one report that Mitchell Sharp actually resigned six months ago, but they haven't figured out yet what he said.

I would be a distracting irritant in the Senate because I speak too fast for them.

I can always win an election on image and good looks alone.

And to the nation's broadcasters, in Toronto, on September 10, 1971:

I made a big hit with Anne Murray — her first big million seller was named after me, "Slowbird."

I don't want to be namedropping in a group like this, because most of you are so much better at it than I am.

It's good to see the heads of CTV and CBC here. I'm sure they watch their own and one another's public affairs specials, and I know they wanted to come here tonight to see what I look like! I hope if they're suitably impressed they might pass it on to the *Globe and Mail*.

I know the CBC will give me the full treatment when I'm

history. I resent the fact that CBC has been covering the Diefenbaker years and calling them "The Tenth Decade." This series should have been called "The Pre-Stanfield Years."

As a keen student of image perception and the slick sell, I tell you that a lot of your advertising stuff is mediocre and old hat.

In the immortal words of Cleopatra, I didn't come here tonight to talk politics.

Finally, to the American Association of Cartoonists, in Ottawa, May 26, 1975:

You've all had about as much to drink as you hoped when you came here, and I think this points up the importance of having realistic goals defined before you call a conference of this kind.

I don't resent being caricatured. Cartoonists get no less pleasure carving me up than they would get carving their own mother. But nobody would pay them to carve up their mothers.

A couple of cartoonists, years ago, tried to prevail on me to enter national politics, and I was flattered until they told me that I had the kind of bony anatomy that they could really do a job on. They said I owed it to my country!

Really, what brought me into national politics was a natural lust for power. You cartoonists have never expressed gratitude for the raw material I've provided.

If it's true that a picture is worth a thousand words, then my calculation in talking to you here tonight is that I am entitled to some 976,000 words in rebuttal. With my rapid-fire delivery it will only take me a few years.

Some cartoonists are still doing cartoons of me with one drooping eyelid. I've had it corrected, and in the interest of those cartoonists who have a passion for symmetry, I've had the other eyelid lowered, and some of you haven't noticed.

The underwear and bananas have been gradually subsiding in your productions. I was getting concerned about underwear being cheapened by overexposure. When people start talking about underwear, I generally tell them to keep their traps shut.

You can never allow your work to be confused by the facts, and I assume that is why your cartoons appear on the editorial pages.

By nature I am a rather serious person, and approach occasions with some sense of mission. The knack for the one-liner just isn't my style.

I have depths and heights you never really bothered to explore, hung up as you are on my eyebrows, and you regard me as a laughable threat to the future of Canada. I'm not really modest at all! I've simply got it all over those other guys.

The only really modest person in federal politics is Mr. Trudeau.

When all is said and done, as the foreman of the crew repairing the septic tank once remarked, "We're all in this together."

How I Love Thee, Uncle Sam

If you grew up in the Maritimes, or the Prairies, or British Columbia, it's hard to be suspicious of the United States, or to worry overmuch about the separate Canadian identity our savants keep prattling about. It's a suspicion that has to be learned, and a hard core of teachers keeps plugging away at it. They get a better hearing in good times, when we're comfy, than in bad times, when we're scared, and most times they keep the juices flowing, especially along the networks of the CBC.

My own feeling is that worrying about the Yanks is not a threat to our identity, it's part of it. After all, it was that concern that led Canada to be founded in the first place, and gave us such things as the Rideau Canal to by-pass hostile Americans. Moncton, New Brunswick, is where it is because the founders wanted the railroad inland and safe from attack, whereas where it really should be is in Shediac-by-the-Sea. And that's why inland Fredericton is the capital of New Brunswick, instead of vulnerable Saint John. And how do you suppose Ottawa got to be the capital of Canada? Because it's sixty miles from the U.S. border, that's how — in those days, as today, that's about as far from that border as anybody in Canada cared to get.

It's hard to be fearful of the States when so many Maritimers headed there and did well, before the border started to tighten up and divert us to Montreal and Toronto. The ones who did well seemed as happy in the United States as they had been in Canada. Maybe happier. Certainly richer. The stay-at-homes envied them, and we admired their big cars when they came home to visit, with their Massachusetts licence plates. In the 1930s one of every five people in what we called the Boston States had a Maritime background, sharing a tradition based on beans, codfish, and clam chowder made with milk, potatoes, and lots of onions.

Having lived for eight postwar years in the United States, I concluded two things — first, that the Americans are much more congenial and appealing on their home turf than when they are abroad; and second, that the lives they lead are very much like our own. The popularity of so much of their culture when it flows across the border bears out how comfortable Canadians are with it, because we can relate so closely to it. Our own achievers in the antic arts drift southward into the U.S. milieu and do well, with nobody noticing the difference.

The question of our separate identity is raised by those who have a vested interest in raising it, and so it becomes basic to our politics, though it has little relation to our everyday lives. The articulate members of our society make the most noise about it, usually to protect their own turf from feared American incursions.

My own love affair with the United States started, I suppose, with having been born there, even though I was brought back to the Maritimes at the age of two weeks and grew up in Saint John, New Brunswick. An early teenage love affair with a visiting Boston tourist named Connie Murphy helped matters — her father was a Saint John émigré who had a fashionable dental practice among the Boston Irish and was a timekeeper at the Boston Garden for the Bruins hockey team. On my visits he would take me to the games. Connie introduced me to Boston society high life, including how to put on a tux. And I introduced myself to the burlesque shows at the Old Howard, without ever laying a glove on Connie.

All roads from Saint John seemed to lead to Boston in those days, or somewhere in the United States. The itinerant dignitaries we interviewed for the local paper were mostly Americans passing through, from Kate Smith to the president of Metropolitan Life, Leroy Lincoln, or the publisher of the Decatur, Illinois, *Herald*, who offered me a job. I had another offer from the Brooklyn *Eagle* at the same time, but decided not to go down that road just yet.

Years later, after Halifax, Vancouver, Montreal, and Toronto, the war and the Nuremberg trials, a spell in Brazil and three years in Ottawa, came the move to New York and eight happy years among the Americans. At first, Connecticut was home, and then New Jersey — northern New Jersey, the most maligned state in the union, and one of the most beautiful.

Maywood was a suburb of Hackensack, one of those "rule of the κ" places that comedians use to get a laugh when all else fails — Brooklyn, Hoboken, Ho Ho Kus, Oshkosh, Waukegan, Winnetka, Saskatoon, Saskatchewan. These were the years when they were building the New York Thruway and the New Jersey Turnpike and the first of the big suburban shopping centres in nearby Paramus. The commuting to Manhattan was on the Susquehanna Railroad to a place called Susquehanna Junction, then change to a bus for the new Port Authority Bus Terminal, that wondrous place built by Robert Moses to replace the old bus turntable in the dingy basement of the Dixie Hotel.

In Manhattan were the offices of Reuters, in the *New York Times* building on 43rd Street, and lunches at the Gaiety Delicatessen and the place we called Dirty Dick's, where the rice pudding was great and the apple pie, like most pie in New York, the best in the world. There were the Wallach drug stores that sold that new wonder, frozen orange juice, and the Horlick's corner stands where the coconut milk went so well with the hot dogs. I still recall celebrating there when I sold the Reuters service to Edward R. Murrow for $35 a week. The clincher was that nobody else had a bureau in Peking, not to mention our coverage of Hillary climbing Everest and Roger Bannister's four-minute mile.

It was the time of McCarthyism, which didn't seem as awful then to those who were looking on as it has come to seem since. It was more a sideshow in the Cold War than a horror show on its own, and watching the senator perform in televised committee hearings was like the wrestling on TV, until Ed Murrow pinpointed the awfulness of it all. The great and good Dwight Eisenhower was president, so nothing terrible could happen, or so I thought, and when they finally brought Joe McCarthy down, we all cheered for the good guys. McCarthy helped make TV what it is today, along with Milton Berle and Ed Sullivan, watched on television screens that had plastic magnifiers to enlarge the six-inch screens. In the daytime, the kids threw blankets over the set and crawled under into the darkness, to sharpen the image of Hopalong Cassidy and Howdy Doody.

I wrote a whole play for the Maywood Home and School PTA about the glories of life in our New Jersey suburb, and we had to remember not to vote in elections because we were landed aliens and not citizens. As den father for our troop of cub scouts I substituted a Canadian Red Ensign for the Stars and Stripes. The neighbourhood kids thought it was great and saluted, until an irate parent objected and insisted on "the real thing," so we had to go and buy one. Taking our flag to a rally, my sons let it fall into the gutter and I said that was no way to treat Old Glory. Son Andrew roared in reply: "You mean Old Stinky!" Nobody heard, thank God.

We survived, and prospered, though Andrew was happy to be sent back to school in Canada, the oldest school on the continent, King's College School in Windsor, Nova Scotia. When he came home to New Jersey after his first term he called me "Sir" getting off the plane, and when I asked him how things had gone he said fine, no excitement. The excitement had been the previous year when half the senior class got expelled for running a still down in the school woods. "They wouldn't have been caught," he said, "except they were selling the stuff to the townspeople and the Mounties saw the lineup." I comforted myself that running a still is part of every Canadian's heritage, at least every Maritimer's.

That same son went on to King's College and Dalhousie University in Halifax and distinguished himself by buying an old hearse to use as a ski bus. When he drove it off the end of a harbour pier in the midst of a driving snowstorm in February, at 2 A.M., he rode it forty feet to the harbour bottom, let it fill, lowered a window, got himself out, and swam to the surface, where he found a dangling cable and pulled himself onto the dock. In the subsequent excitement he told a reporter that he reckoned it wasn't his time to die, and the dispatch went around the world. Ever since, I have been known in Halifax as Andrew Lynch's father.

It was in New Jersey that son Blake developed baseball skills of a high order, only to be diagnosed as a leukemia sufferer with a hole in his enlarged heart, whereupon he gave his possessions away and said goodbye to all. He recovered, his athletic career prospered in baseball and football, he won many an argument with his fists, and sits today as a provincial court judge in New Brunswick, occasionally attending school reunions in New Jersey, where he has the time of his life.

And all through those years we had the renewal of old but still fresh war correspondent friendships, with Lionel Shapiro making his fortune writing novels and Walter Cronkite gaining the recognition that would serve him well and last so long.

Shapiro, who had covered the war for *Maclean's* and the North American Newspaper Alliance, burst into my New York office one day to announce he had, in his pocket, his first advance cheque from Paramount Pictures for movie rights to the novel he was still writing, *The Sixth of June*. "We must tell Ralph," he exclaimed.

So I put in a call to Ralph Allen, then editor of *Maclean's* in Toronto, and when Ralph came on the line I said Shapiro was there and had some news. Shapiro told Allen the tidings, waving in the air the cheque for $25,000, and after the two of them had talked for a while Allen asked that I come back on the line.

"Am I correct in my impression," he said, "that this is a collect call?"

I said it was.

"A collect call," said Allen, "to tell me that Shapiro has just got a cheque for $25,000 from Paramount?"

Quite so. Long pause.

"You know what I think?" mused Allen. "I think our boy will go far!"

He did, too, until cancer caught up with him, and he died in the Royal Victoria Hospital in Montreal, dictating his last thoughts into a new-fangled tape machine that Allen had sent him in hopes that something memorable might result. Nothing did. But *The Sixth of June* made a fine movie, as good in its way as *The Longest Day*, which came years later. On the strength of it, a bunch of us former war correspondents got on the Ed Sullivan Show, and that was the start of my TV career.

As for Cronkite, he moved to New York from Washington, where he had made a mark as the local newscaster for CBS, and soon the money started rolling in and he came under the financial management of a genius named Nathan Bienstalk. Bienstalk insisted that all of Walter's money go through his hands — salary, special fees, everything — and he would dole out living expenses to Walter and Betsy Cronkite, investing the rest and taking care of the tax angles.

One day I visited Walter at a beach house he was renting on the Jersey shore, and he said he was consumed with guilt. A cheque for $1500 had been sent to him by mistake, instead of to Bienstalk. It was for presiding at the opening of a supermarket, and it had arrived on Friday, and here it was Sunday. I said there didn't seem to be any problem, just give the cheque to Bienstalk on Monday. Walter looked crestfallen.

"I can't," he said. "I spent it."

On what?

"Come and see," he said, and led me into the side yard of the cottage, where there was a bright red Austin Healey sports car.

"I just walked into the dealership at Red Bank where they sell these things," said Walter, "and asked what he had for $1500. They came up with this, and it's great, and Betsy and I spent the rest of the day tooling all around the countryside having a ball."

So Walter decided to face Bienstalk, who was furious and threatened to resign the account, but he didn't. He had to suffer through the subsequent years in which Cronkite pursued a side career as an amateur sports-car racing driver, all because that one cheque went astray.

It was one of many friendships that made the New York years memorable, and gave me a love for that city, and that country, that has stayed with me ever since. And when it came time to come home, the road lay through the United Nations and the job there of CBC correspondent, engineered by George Ferguson, the editor of the *Montreal Star*, who wanted me to write a UN column for the paper and who thought he could get the CBC interested. When he did, he phoned me in great excitement to say "the fuck's on!"

And all through these grand years there had been Willie Mays with the Giants at the Polo Grounds, Bobby Thompson's home run, the Dodgers with Jackie Robinson and Roy Campanella, and going to the hockey games at the old Madison Square Garden, cheering for Gump Worsley and Andy Bathgate and joining the New York fans in roaring at the referee, "Storey is a bum!" The fans that sat around us all thought hockey was a phoney, just a step up from wrestling but preferable to basketball, so they kept coming, though I could never get used to the habit of leaving the rink five minutes before the end of the game, whatever the score. Everybody wanted to get out of the parking lot and beat the traffic to the Holland Tunnel or the George Washington Bridge.

Every soul I ever knew in the world came to visit and to see the town, and they never ceased to marvel. British publishers came to ask me about that upstart Roy Thomson who was creating a stir in Britain, "but he'll never make the club, old boy!" Thomson himself had told me he would, because after his first study of the newspaper business in Britain he came to his most vital conclusion: "They're all so God damn stupid!"

And my old wartime colleague Matt Halton came to town from London with his son David in tow, and David talked like every proper young British schoolboy who's gone to the right schools, and Matthew took him to a baseball game at Ebbetts Field where they saw, he said, Black Joe pitch.

"Not Black Joe," I corrected, "Joe Black."

"He was beautiful," said Matt. David just looked bemused, dreaming no doubt of cricket, and Matt said he'd take him to the old home in Pincher Creek, Alberta, and introduce him to the real life. Listening to David now, he must have found it.

Wartime memories were greener then and I could talk to Matt and Shap and Ralph about things we had seen and times we had known, not all of them facing the foe. Shapiro liked to recall the late summer of 1944, behind the battle lines, in Lille. We had taken over a former German headquarters as our press camp at Fouquambert, known irreverently as Fuck You with a Cucumber. One night I dropped Ross Munro's four-battery flashlight, a presentation from the grateful bosses of Canadian Press, into the very deep-dug privy, and Ross had to visit that privy for the following three days and four nights, aware that his faithful light was glowing below, beyond rescue but bravely shining.

Another time, Shapiro asked me to arrange a night on the town — which I did at what was reputedly the hottest whore-house in Lille. Leading our party of Shapiro, Ralph Allen, and Matt Halton, I knocked on the door, though Shapiro was the first to enter. He was greeted by a buxom woman who locked him in hot embrace and, at the same time, wielded a knife on his belt, slicing it in two and sending his trousers sliding down below his knees. "You want action," I said, "you got it!" But the scene was so unnerving to my companions that they lost all desire. Shapiro pulled up his pants and we went back to the press camp, undefiled, and ate a big salami that had been sent to Lionel by a fan in Montreal.

And when we got to Brussels came the great love of Shapiro's life, the one he never ceased talking about, and the one that, if not unrequited, was never consummated. Gertrude Lawrence. Honestly.

Shapiro was always stage struck, from the days when he first went to Manhattan to write a column for the *Montreal Gazette* called Lights and Shadows of Broadway and became a protégé of Walter Winchell. Shap used to talk about showgirls he had known and loved, but none of us believed him even though he could provide names, dates, dimensions, and performance figures of an explicit nature. But of love he knew nothing, until he saw Gertrude Lawrence entertain the troops in Brussels. He went backstage and paid court to her, to the extent that when the show finished its run she stayed on in Brussels to be with Shapiro, following which he went back to London every chance he got, to be with her. He brought her to the war correspondents' mess at the Canterbury Hotel and they did the town together. Shapiro was, for the first and only time in his life, starry eyed, and we were glad for him. It came to nothing in the end and Gertrude Lawrence returned to her naval officer husband in the United States. Shapiro visited them from time to time, still carrying his torch and vowing to immortalize the romance in prose. He never did, but he talked about her to the day he died.

Matt Halton and I had more recent adventures to talk about, because for him the whole of life was an adventure, and it didn't end with the war, though that was the greatest.

More on Matt, and Ralph, and Philip

After the war, Matt refused the blandishments of Canadian socialists who wanted him to return to Canada and run for Parliament, capitalizing not only on his fame but on the touch of pink that was part of his nature, as it was, and is, of all good CBC commentators. He stayed in London, continuing his broadcasts for the CBC, making a name on the BBC, and moving in a circle that included the Thursday Club.

In the summer of 1950, when Halton invited me to have lunch with him at the Thursday Club, I had never heard of the institution, but I assumed it would be something unusual, knowing him. After all, not five years before, Halton and I had been having drinks in the American Bar of the Savoy Hotel, in company with Christopher Buckley of the *Daily Telegraph* and O'Dowd Gallagher of the *Daily Express*, and we kept drinking beyond the closing time for dinner in the Savoy Grill. Halton said not to worry, he was so well known at the Savoy that he would be able to get us some food, so he crossed the bar room and disappeared from sight down the grand staircase leading to the main lobby.

When he failed to return, Buckley said that nobody knew the Savoy better than he did, so he disappeared around the corner and down the stairs — and he didn't come back. "Have no fear," said Gallagher, "I am better known at the Savoy than anybody. I shall go and find our companions, organize some dinner, and come back and fetch you." So off he went around the corner and down the stairs — and he failed to return.

"Well," said I to our three female companions, "I know nothing about the Savoy but I shall go and see what happened to the three of them and I shall return with tidings." So off I went around the corner and there, at the foot of the stairs, was a mob scene in the lobby of the Savoy, with people milling about and shouting, and a ring of policemen, and there in the centre of it all were Halton, Buckley, and Gallagher.

I descended the broad staircase and approached the edge of the crowd, asking a frock-coated hotel employee what was going on. "Do you know these people?" he asked with that curl of the lip that only functionaries in hotels like the Savoy can summon up when expressing contempt.

"Yes," I said. "Can I be of assistance?"

"They," he said with obvious distaste, "are being removed from the premises. And if you are with them, you are, too."

"Can you tell me the problem?"

"Out!"

I won enough time to return upstairs and fetch our companions, who returned to the lobby with me, and the seven of us were escorted out to the fabled, Rolls-encrusted courtyard that fronts the main entrance to the Savoy and bade never to darken their door again. When we trudged along the Strand I observed that whatever happened to any of us, for the rest of our lives, we could always say "we've been thrown out of better places than this," since in most quarters it is agreed that there is no better place than the Savoy.

I asked Halton what had happened, and he said it was all a terrible accident. It seemed that the moment he turned down the stairs and was lost from our view, he tripped over his feet, lost his balance, and rolled down the staircase, at the very moment when the Dowager Duchess of Devonshire was ascending. Matthew caught her in mid flight, so to speak, and rolled her body up with his, the two of them landing in the lobby in a mass of flying arms and legs.

Now, well-connected as Halton may have been in the hotel, the Duchess had an edge on him. When she had caught her breath sufficiently to give vent to her indignation, she marshalled the full sympathy of the hotel staff, who summoned the constabulary, and the more Halton pleaded his innocence the worse his position became. Once Buckley arrived to help he was swept into the net, and so was Gallagher, and so, in the end, was I. For the rest of his days Halton pleaded his innocence in the matter, saying anybody could trip on a staircase and it was a wonder he didn't suffer serious injury. Besides, why did she have to be a duchess, for God's sake?

It was years before I ventured near the Savoy again, and when I did a strange thing happened that led to their putting my picture up on one of their walls. The occasion was a postwar return to London of the Canadian War Correspondents Association, and a decision by Ralph Allen and me that we should attend the Derby at Epsom Downs.

I agreed to lay on the refreshments and informed my Savoy floor waiter that I would be needing a hamper for the Derby. He said to leave everything to him, and would I be requiring him to lay out my clothes, sir? No, I would not, as he must have known from the most cursory inspection of my wardrobe, devoid as it was of topper, frock coat, or any of the other accoutrements that customarily accompany a Savoy hamper to the races.

In the morning, dressed in a flaming red sports shirt and blue jeans, I buzzed for my man and he eyed me with just the faintest trace of disapproval. When I asked for my hamper he said it would await me in the lobby. I thanked him and went below, to find an array of hampers stacked inside the very doors through which Halton and the rest of us had been expelled. Assorted chauffeurs and footmen were picking up the hampers as directed by their splendidly attired masters, and it was with a furtive air that I searched for my hamper and, having found it, carried it outside to await Allen's arrival. His part of the deal was to scrounge an army staff car and driver, which arrived in due course amid the Rolls and Daimlers that clogged the courtyard, and in I got with my giant hamper and away we went to Epsom.

Upon arrival we discovered that the most difficult thing to do at Epsom is to see a horse race. The crowd lines the course about fifty deep and, unless you are in the front row, all you see are the tops of the jockeys' caps. The Derby was the fourth race

Ralph Allen and I view the Derby from an Epsom ferris wheel in 1960, while feasting on our hamper from the Savoy. The colonies strike back! Courtesy *The Calgary Herald*.

on the program and it was obvious that if we were going to see the race, and find a comfortable place to attack the Savoy hamper, we had to take fast action.

There was an amusement park close to the track and it had a ferris wheel. I suggested to Allen that possibly we could see something from the top of that. "We might," he said, "but it would be hard to follow the race and swallow the food if we were going round and round." We hit on the idea of leasing the wheel for the entire period of the big race, and when we asked the operator he was delighted, since nobody ever bought a ticket until the Derby was over. So it was that we paid him £5 each and, minutes before the race, we climbed aboard the deserted wheel and he lifted us to the top. We had a view of the entire racecourse from beginning to end, plus a good look from above at all the top-hatted toffs in the enclosure.

We opened the hamper and gasped in wonderment. First came the Savoy linen, two pink-on-pink damask napkins and a small tablecloth. Then the sterling silver cutlery, masses of it. Then two roast quail. Salad in a Spode bowl, and dressing in a Waterford crystal cruet. A Melton Mowbray pie. A trifle in a cut-glass bowl, with goblets to match. A bottle of choice claret, with a silver corkscrew and two long-stemmed glasses. Four bottles of ale, and two steins with silver lids. A loaf of crisp bread, with cutting board and knife. Choice oranges, apples, bananas, and grapes. Hard cheese, soft cheese, a jar of Stilton, and assorted table wafers.

Swaying high above the crowd the two of us fell upon this repast, pausing only to toss quail bones over our shoulders. We observed the start of the race, and the whole of its progress, and we were the only ones in the crowd of 200,000 to do so. By the time the ferris wheel proprietor wound us down to the ground we had demolished most of the contents of the hamper and counted our ten quid well spent.

When I put "rental of ferris wheel" on my expense account our Southam company treasurer in Toronto was kind enough to telephone his congratulations for thinking up an item that no correspondent in his experience had ever devised before. And the *Calgary Herald*'s cartoon of our caper wound up on the wall of the Savoy Press Office. Southam's never did find out about the cost of that hamper, which was astronomical, but never was the company's money put to better use.

When I got back to the Savoy that evening I stretched myself out in one of those giant tubs the British do so well, and picked up the telephone that was beside the bath to telephone colleagues and tell them of our adventure. The cord of the telephone dropped into my bath water and I found myself being electrocuted. I threw the instrument onto the bathroom floor, jumped from the tub and pressed the button marked valet, and when he arrived in fifteen seconds (summons at the Savoy are always answered in fifteen seconds) I complained that I had very nearly been electrocuted. He said there must be a terrible mistake because the telephone was supposed to be beside the WC so one could take incoming calls when otherwise engaged. He summoned the maintenance people and in fifteen seconds they were there and moved the telephone from beside the tub to beside the loo.

Ten years earlier, in 1950, at Matt Halton's suggestion, I had stayed at the Devereux, a pub off the Strand that had just been reopened after having been gutted in the Blitz. The ancient inn had been completely reconstructed with modern touches all through its innards, and it was reputed to have the best dining room in the Fleet Street area.

The bathroom on the top floor had one of those big tubs that the English, despite their failure to grasp the finer points of twentieth-century plumbing, continued to turn out until they finally got the word about bathing in the fetal position. Austerity was still rigid, and one of its provisions was that nobody could use more than two inches of bath water in the tub. At the Devereux, we were told that the tub had a secret device that would detect any violation of the two-inch waterline, so I obeyed the edict scrupulously, even though it meant no luxuriating in the body-length tub.

One morning, though, I succumbed. It was chilly, and the day before I had scored a minor triumph at the office, saving the *Chicago Tribune* contract for Reuters, so I decided I deserved a real bath. I ran the water until it was a foot deep and climbed in, stretched full out, and floated blissfully. I wallowed about, soaping and splashing, and after half an hour I rose from the suds, towelled down and dressed, descending from the top floor with a song on my lips and nary a trace of guilt in my heart.

The middle floor of the inn contained the dining room and the kitchen, and on the landing a reception committee awaited me — the landlord, his wife, and the cook — all Swiss, and all very angry. The chef's tall white hat was soaking wet and drooped down over his face, and the rest of him was soaked, too.

The manager spoke: "Did you enjoy your bath, sir?"

"Why, yes," I answered brightly, "yes I did, very much, thank you."

"The chef," said the manager, "shared the experience with you, but without much joy."

"I don't understand," I said, taken aback.

"Step this way, sir," said the manager, walking towards the kitchen.

Once there, he pointed to the newly plastered ceiling, at a spot over the giant stove.

"You see that spout up there?" he asked.

"Whatever is it?" I stalled.

"We didn't know what it was ourselves," he said. "In fact, we had never noticed it until your bath brought it to our chef's attention."

He went on: "When the reconstruction was being finished, the government people came in and did something about the plumbing but they didn't say what — just that they had installed an overflow system that would create a nuisance if anybody used more than the legal two inches of water in the tub. You, sir, are the first to do so. When you lay back in the tub the overflow poured out on top of the chef."

The chef bowed stiffly, my bathwater dripping off the end of his ample nose. I gave my profuse apologies and offered to buy the cook a drink, or a new hat, or anything, but he waved me off. I asked what I could do to put matters right, and the manager laughed. "Obey the law," he said sternly. "But just in case, we're sticking a bung in the end of that pipe!"

But I started out to tell about Matthew Halton and his invitation to lunch with him at the Thursday Club. He gave me the address, and when I got there it turned out to be Wheeler's Old Oyster House on Old Compton Street in Soho. The building is four storeys high and very narrow, with rooms on each floor for the diners. Halton had left my name with Mr. Walsh, the proprietor, so when I identified myself I was led up the three flights of narrow stairs and into the topmost room, where a board was spread that was very festive, considering it was 1950 and there was still austerity in Britain.

The assembled guests were even more impressive, and Matthew made the introductions with the same aplomb as when he had introduced me to his old pal Ernest Hemingway in Mont St. Michel after our break-out from the Normandy beachhead in the summer of 1944.

"This is Prince Philip."

"This is his aide, Michael Parker."

"This is James Robertson Justice."

"This is Baron, the photographer."

And there were others whose names went by in a blur, including the editor of the *Daily Express* and the owner of the Arsenal Football Club.

I noted that everybody had a big leather medal strung around his neck, bearing the inscription "Battle of Wheeler's, 1950." I was informed that the medals had been bestowed that very day by the host, that the battle had taken place at a meeting of the Thursday Club two weeks previously, and that Wheeler's had been closed for renovations for most of the intervening time.

The host was kind enough to tell me the story. The members of the club were gathered in the upstairs room, even as today, awaiting the announcement of the cuckoo on the wall that it was one o'clock, which was the traditional signal for the luncheon to commence. At a previous meeting, a challenge had been issued to Baron that the cuckoo kooked "one" too fast for him to get a photograph of it. So Baron brought in his biggest bellows camera, one of those sway-backed, six-feet-long jobs, and he set it up aimed at the clock on the wall, and when it was a minute to one he got in under the black cloth cape at the back end of the camera and tensed himself for the moment of truth.

No sooner had Baron gone into his tent than Michael Parker produced, from his pockets, a number of thunderflashes, which are the explosives that are used to simulate bombs and shell-bursts in war games and war movies. He handed them out and, just when it seemed time for the cuckoo to emerge, Parker threw his thunderflash under Baron and blew him up, camera and all. At the same moment, James Robertson Justice, the distinguished bewhiskered film actor, threw his flash under the table containing the lunch, and blew the whole meal to thunder-ation. And Prince Philip, with the wicked eye for which he was noted then and now, dashed over to the fireplace and threw his thunderflash up the flue, where it went off with a terrible crash, resulting in a deluge of soot that turned the entire room black, and all the people in it.

The proprietor ran downstairs to reassure the paying guests on the floor below, only to find that all the fireplaces — every room had them — had disgorged clouds of soot and that all his patrons were black, together with their clothes, their food, and their attitudes.

Problem: How to mollify them, and think up an explana-tion that did not involve telling them that the agent of their misfortune was the husband of Princess Elizabeth?

It wasn't easy, but they smuggled Philip out by way of the fire escape and adjoining rooftops, the rest of the Thursday Club wags followed the same route, and the patrons were told they would be indemnified. The club members chipped in to help with the damages, and everybody was happy with his medal.

The luncheon I was attending was less eventful than the one just described, but was rollicking fun. It was a farewell party for Philip, who was leaving the following day for Malta to pick up his first naval command, the frigate *Magpie*. He did a very creditable Charlie Chaplin imitation and sang a calypso about the touring West Indies cricket team that had just defeated England, thanks to the enchanted bowling of "those two very good friends of mine, Rhamadin and Valentine."

I have met Philip several times since but I mentioned the Thursday Club incident to him only once, and he frosted over. I got the impression he had never heard of any of those chaps, including Halton.

One of the joys for those of us who knew and loved Matt Halton has been to see his son David following his old man's career pattern in broadcasting. David has less of the Thespian in him than Matthew had, which is perhaps just as well in these less adventurous times. The black and whites of war, the good and evil of democracy versus Nazism, were meat and drink to the father, while the son has had to deal with the complexities of peace, or little wars without heroes and stirring battle cries.

David Halton has a lot of his father's humour and a good deal of his mother's wide-ranging sanity, and some of his best stories are about travelling abroad with Canadian prime ministers, covering for the CBC. Here he is on Trudeau's epic three-week tour of the Far East in January 1983. *Halton*:

Trudeau took off on this trip, theoretically to drum up more Canadian trade with the countries of the Pacific Rim but really, because this wasn't a subject that he had seemed to care a great deal about before, to get himself out of the country. We went to Brunei and such places, where there wasn't much trade. We arrived in Bangkok, and Trudeau's staff assured us that the prime minister had this extraordinarily packed schedule and that he would be working his ass off during those three weeks. And then Trudeau just disappeared.

I ran into an old friend from the embassy and he asked me if I had heard that Trudeau was going to a big Thai kick-boxing match that night with little Sasha. He said he wouldn't tell me any more about it because it was such a big secret. So I wandered up to the concièrge in our hotel and asked if there was any kick-boxing going on, and he said there was, just down the street a couple of blocks, at 8 o'clock. So along I went with the CBC camera crew and, shortly thereafter, Trudeau came in with Sasha, and he got all excited during the bouts. There were great shots of him having fun.

Next morning the word got around the press corps that we had all this great footage and everybody got sore and demanded similar access in future. But more importantly, all the coverage swung around to criticism of Trudeau for enjoying himself at the taxpayers' expense. He, in turn, accused the media brigade of being in the fleshpots. Things got worse and worse, to the point where Trudeau came out with that famous remark that made all the headlines back in Canada: "I'm working hard here, and if I want to take some hours off why shouldn't I? After all, at this time of year most Canadians are either skiing in the Rockies or on some beach in the Caribbean." This, of course, was when employment was at 12 per cent and the economy was going to the pits.

Trudeau then went to Mount Fuji and took in the Sumo wrestling in Japan. So far as we could determine he never did sell anything or make any trade deals. He kept saying that government-to-government contacts were essential, that we shouldn't expect him to come out with any hard deals, and that he was just preparing the ground. There was a great picture, though, of him wearing a coolie hat in some obscure wadi.

I interjected here that stories like that about Trudeau tended to endear him to Canadians, rather than giving offence. Joe Clark couldn't get away with it, and we're still waiting to see how Mulroney makes out. Our song about this Trudeau trip went:

> In the fleshpots of Bankok,
> We drank whiskey by the crock,
> While he worked his bleeding ass off,
> Selling wheat around the clock!

Halton: Mulroney's people are so obsessed by the lessons of those trips, and the media getting bored on long travels, that they have a policy of Mulroney never going anywhere for more than two weeks. And wherever he goes, his people pack in engagements day and night. On his first Paris trip we thought it might be a pleasant week, but they made him look busy at a lot of spurious events such as visiting Canadian student residences, so no one would write stories about him gallivanting the way Trudeau used to do. In fact, Trudeau may have queered the pitch for generations of prime ministers to come.

I should add that when Trudeau worked, he did work quite hard.

Somebody's Got to Live in Saskatchewan!

John Diefenbaker told a story about when, as a young politician, he was admitted to the federal penitentiary at Prince Albert to address the inmates. Not that they were able to vote, as he explained, but at least they might provide an audience, not an easy thing for a Tory to get in Saskatchewan in those days.

"It is good to see so many of you here," was his opening line.

"Considering all the other things you could be doing," he went on. Titters in the audience.

"The other places you could be...."

"I want your support in my work, as you have my support in yours. I know you have gone through a lot to get where you are."

By this time, roars from the crowd of convicts.

Things went from bad to worse, and Diefenbaker wound up with a flourish that, as he himself said, finished him off.

"Let men of conviction work together for liberty, equality, and freedom in this great Canada of ours!" Loud cheers.

Later on, Diefenbaker mastered the art of turning misfortune to his advantage, but he never reached the heights he perceived in his idol, Sir John A. Diefenbaker loved to tell the story about the time Sir John went to a country confrontational meeting with an opponent and had to take a fifteen-mile sleigh ride to get there. Huddled beneath the furs, Sir John nibbled on a bottle of gin and was well warmed when he got to the meeting hall.

The meeting was already in progress, and his opponent was speaking. Sir John swept into the hall and headed for the platform, when the heat of the wood stove and the smell of the crowd hit him. He stopped in the aisle and threw up, shocking the crowd into silence. Finally, he looked up, drew a deep breath, and said: "I am sorry, ladies and gentlemen, but the sound of my opponent's voice invariably has this effect upon me!" The crowd cheered.

Judy LaMarsh was better at telling stories on other people than on herself, but one she told was about addressing a meeting in rural Saskatchewan, when Grits were even less popular than Tories had been in John Diefenbaker's youth. The subject of LaMarsh's speech was the agriculture policy of the Pearson government, and during one pause for breath she heard a farmer on one side of the hall mutter: "Bet she's never been behind a plough!" And from the other side of the hall came the response: "Looks like she should be in front of one!"

It was Judy, too, who claimed to have heard a woman get up at a western rally where bilingualism was being discussed, and shout: "If English was good enough for Jesus, it's good enough for me!"

Judy liked Diefenbaker better than she liked her fellow Liberal Pierre Trudeau — "that bastard," in her words. I had my own affection for Diefenbaker, but he wasn't my favourite Saskatchewaner. Don Minifie was.

Why so many media giants have come from Saskatchewan is something that has puzzled those of us who regard the Maritimes as the prime producers of fine journalists, followed closely by Manitoba. Winnipeg has an intellectual ambience of its own that has long propelled its graduates east and west, to the principal benefit of Vancouver and Toronto. The same can be said for products of Halifax, Saint John, and Charlottetown, who followed the roads east and south to success.

But why Saskatchewan?

Pondering this riddle, I am reminded of an episode in the club car of the transcontinental train "The Canadian," climbing westward into the Rocky Mountains. A loudmouthed British Columbian had been holding forth to the rest of us about the superiority of his province, and expressing pity for those who lived elsewhere. When we crossed the Great Divide and entered British Columbia, he jumped to his feet and exclaimed: "Look at it! Isn't it grand? Isn't it beautiful? Why would anybody want to live anyplace else?" And he whirled on a quiet-spoken woman from Saskatchewan, who had tried vainly to get a word in earlier, and demanded: "Why would anybody want to live in Saskatchewan?"

There was a long pause, and then she said, with a defiant air, "Somebody's got to live in Saskatchewan, that's why!"

There were many media people from Saskatchewan. J. B. McGeachy, who once gave up a Rhodes Scholarship for the unrequited love of a maid, went on to lay waste to ignorance wherever he encountered it, at home and abroad. He was the only man I have ever seen who, when hired to appear on television, could make producers and directors whimper with terror, tempered by admiration. "They like to kick us around to make themselves comfortable," he once confided to me on a CBC year-end show, just before he levelled me on air for calling Charles de Gaulle a fascist. "We are the ones who should be comfortable. The talent. To hell with them!" For me, taught like all talent to treat everybody in studio with deference, this was marvellous heresy. And McGeachy, blind as a bat and not giving a damn, was right.

It was in that same Toronto studio I encountered another product of Saskatchewan, Jeanne Sauvé, at the height of her own career as a television personality, dazzling then as now. I played "Un Canadien Errant" for her on the harmonica and she said that lovely song always made her cry. So she cried.

There came to newspapers, mostly in the East, Don McGillivray from Moose Jaw and Bill MacPherson from Moosomin. Also Lamont Tilden, Jack McArthur, Ronald Anderson, Wayne Chevaldayoff, Peter Dempson, Ron Poulton, and wee Allan Fotheringham, who grew up in British Columbia but still gets misty-eyed and mushy-penned when he thinks of his Saskatchewan beginnings. And big brained, big eyed Pamela Wallin. Ralph Allen, the mighty Rufus of the *Globe and Mail*, *Maclean's*, the *Toronto Star*, and all his books, good and bad, became so distinguished they have a museum in his home town dedicated to his memory. That place in Ox Bow moves me as much as the Matthew Halton High School in Pincher Creek, Alberta, commemorating that other well-remembered giant of our trade from sodbusting country.

Thus has Saskatchewan sent her best into the journalistic fray, to the national enrichment. And while doing this, she gave us such sinews of nationhood as the Regina Riots, the Regina Manifesto, the first socialist government in North America, Tommy Douglas, John Diefenbaker, the Thatchers, M. J. Coldwell, Tommy Shoyama, Art Linkletter. And my own favourite, James M. Minifie, one of the smartest journalists who ever lived, and one of the sexiest bald-headed, one-eyed men ever to tread the boards.

For the CBC, Minifie covered Washington as though it were enemy territory, though he was always comfortable there and, with his artist wife, shared a small mansion in Georgetown which was one of the city's most coveted salons. The CBC did programs on Minifie's Washington, as though he owned the town, and Canadians lapped it up, especially when he was socking it to the Yanks. He was an apostle of Canadian independence with fire in his belly, and so strong a suspicion of American motives that the CIA and FBI had him on their hit list, or so he himself imagined.

Minifie kept coming back to Canada to cover elections, make speeches, and tour in support of his published tracts, notably *Peacemaker or Powder Monkey*, in which he preached an end to our military alliances with the United States. And if people thought it strange that the Washington correspondent of the CBC should be taking such a line, nobody said so, at least not publicly, so great was Minifie's stature and so powerful his presence. He came home without ever moving home, and re-established his Canadian identity from Washington.

He coloured the thinking of his time, the 1950s and 1960s, and spiced in among his reports from the United States were recollections of his Saskatchewan boyhood and his pride in the fact that the previous owners of the family farmlands in Saskatchewan were Stone Age people. He became one of our first celebrity electronic journalists. The CBC had a much stronger hold on the eyes and ears of the nation then than now, and the number of people appearing on air was much smaller. Hence their identities were more vivid than in today's media mob scenes.

Minifie packed halls from coast to coast when he made his

lecture tours, and his one good eye would gleam when attractive women were around him, whether questioning his views or agreeing with them. He had a quick eye for a dollar. One of the things that cemented our friendship was when I was the CBC correspondent at the United Nations, and was doing a column on the side for the biggest newspaper in Brazil, *O Estado do Sao Paolo*. I suggested they take a Washington column from Minifie, which they did. Both of us simply hived off the stuff we were sending to Canada, which suited the Brazilians just fine, and it brought in a lot of cruzeiros.

And wherever Minifie went, he would break away from whatever he was doing, socializing or working, to make what he called his "sends" to CBC radio, always ending with the stretched-out signature, "This is James M. Minifie, in Washing-ton," or wherever he happened to be. All of it in the clipped Rhodes Scholar Oxford accent that didn't sound a bit like Saskatchewan. He once broke away from coverage of a Canadian election to do the first papal visit to New York, and was broadcasting live to the nation with the United Nations building as a backdrop. Minifie was fresh from the hustings in Quebec, but he gave the item on His Holiness in Manhattan all the eloquence he could muster, winding up with this flourish: "This is James M. Minifie, in Chi-cou-ta-mi!"

He and I used to vie for the biggest audiences on the Canadian Club speaking circuit, and I think he usually won, especially with the women's clubs. We shared a secret hope that one day we might encounter the sex-crazed president of a Women's Canadian Club, who would carry the visiting speaker off to her secret den of lust where she would violate us, as the song says, in the vilest way that she knew. It never did happen to me, in an estimated 250 Canadian Club appearances. I don't think it ever happened to Minifie, either, though he was more aggressive than I and had a visible effect on women. He liked to spice his conversations with sexy terms, a glint in his one good eye.

I don't know where the notion of the sex-crazed hostess came from, but I think it had something to do with the stream of English lecturers who used to come to Canada before the war and freeload on the clubs in every city during leisurely coast-to-coast tours. Some, like Oscar Wilde, did it for the money, but others did it for the honour and pleasure of the thing, and for decades very few Canadian speakers could get a word in, so thick were the British on the ground. One such visitor was the early Winston Churchill, who was reputed to have the hots for a young woman at Rideau Hall, in the entourage of the Governor General. His pursuit was unsuccessful, though he was a wow on the platform.

At that time there were Canadian Clubs in every city and town, a tradition that continued until well into the 1960s, by which time Canadian speakers had begun to displace the British, who found the freeload pickings had turned thin. The going fees were $25 per speech, and you travelled by train and bus. On one tour of Ontario I made seventeen speeches in twelve days, while on the Prairies it was fourteen speeches in ten days, and in British Columbia fifteen speeches in nine days, including a sleep in the hotel bathtub in Revelstoke to escape the cockroaches. The biggest hazard of the tours was the reputation I had for liking brownies, and the mounds of them that greeted me at every reception. And usually, when they talked about other speakers, they mentioned Minifie as often as they did Charlotte Whitton.

I remember Minifie most vividly during the election campaign of 1963, when we were touring with the Liberal campaign of Mike Pearson. Minifie despaired, as we all did, of Pearson's habit of taking a hot hall, an audience that had been warmed up by the local speakers, and then cooling it out by making a flat speech. There was a meeting in Moncton and Louis Robichaud, the premier of New Brunswick, had warmed up the crowd as only Louis could when he was at the top of his form. He had them screaming, and drew a standing ovation when he introduced Pearson. We waited for the usual letdown, but it didn't come. Pearson made a short, snappy speech, and it was terrific, bringing the crowd to its feet at the end. Everybody went home happy, and during the walk back to the hotel with Minifie I said, "Don, that's the best he's ever been."

"Ya," said Minifie with a chuckle, "I think he smells pussy."

On that same visit to the Maritimes, Minifie did a memorable broadcast, breaking new ground in television election reporting. He was sitting on the bow of a fishing dory, and the camera shot him with his feet dangling over the side, rocking back and forth with the sea in the background. What didn't show was that we had the dory propped on a wooden log, and I was at the stern pumping it up and down. The effect was terrific, including the creaking of the rigging.

I attended parties with Minifie in Moncton, Regina, Winnipeg, and Edmonton, usually with beer-hall crowds that he seemed to enjoy more than the society bunch. Once, in San Francisco for the Republican convention that nominated Barry Goldwater, we went to a night club and they called for volunteers to take part in a panel show. Both Minifie and I were veterans of panel shows on CBC, so we trooped up on stage, where we were joined by a woman in a flowing evening dress. As she explained the rules, she would dance about the stage and our job was to yank panels of material off her dress. We took turns, and bits and pieces of the dress came away, until finally there was only one piece left, covering her vitals, and Minifie removed it with a flourish that brought cheers from the now aroused audience.

It was on that trip that, when we went to the airport for the return journey, we encountered Duncan MacPherson in the airport lobby. MacPherson, Canada's most famous political cartoonist, had set up his materials and was working away amid the airport throngs, oblivious to all that was going on around him. I clapped him on the shoulder and said how great it was to see a real artist so taken up with his work that he could do it in a busy airport.

"Work, hell," grumped MacPherson. "I missed my flight yesterday and what I'm doing here is altering my ticket to today's date so they won't notice. Damned hard work to do it right because you see I have to do it on each sheet, and match the colours and everything."

He got away with it, but I've always classed it as a gross misuse of genius.

At home in Washington, Minifie was more inclined to be on his dignity. After a massive stroke he was treated with tender loving care by his wife in their magnificently furnished Georgetown abode. His recovery was very slow, his speech was slurred, and for a long time he could totter only from one room to another. Finally he said he felt well enough to attempt the walk to the corner store for some cigarettes. He ambled away, and once around the corner hailed a cab, went to the airport and caught a plane to Toronto, where he showed up at the door of his longtime young lover. She took him in and propped him among her collection of teddy bears. As soon as they could, the two of them flew to Victoria, where Minifie owned a house that he had bought for his late mother. They moved in, and it was there that Minifie spent the rest of his life in apparent bliss, marred only by his conviction that CIA agents were after him.

That famous voice never did recover its cadence, but he was able to lecture at the University of Victoria and to enjoy life in lotus land, combing the beaches for firewood and evolving a strange theory that the annual springtime burst of leaves on trees in the Northern Hemisphere changed the profile of the earth and altered the speed of its revolutions. I never could grasp the meaning of this, or share his excitement over it, but it gave him great satisfaction in his terminal years.

Sticking the Country Together

The things that hold this funny country together are quite comical in themselves, provided you aren't part of them and thus can look at them with a clear head and an untrammelled mind. They are, in order of their own self-importance, the Canadian Broadcasting Corporation, the Toronto *Globe and Mail*, *Maclean's*, Air Canada, Canadian National and Canadian Pacific, the Trans-Canada Highway, and our national news agency, the Canadian Press. I refrain from including Pierre Berton and Peter C. Newman for fear of being accused of sour grapes, or jeopardizing all the research and development jobs they create before they take pen in hand. And I omit the welfare programs, such as Petro-Canada, the pogey, baby bonuses, and other examples of patriotism by the buck.

The CBC, Air Canada, and CN are known respectively as the People's Network, the People's Airline, and the People's Railway, having been so dubbed by me following a return from the People's Republic of China in 1965. These terms soon passed into common usage, and in the case of the CBC, the description was shortened to "the Peeps," the way the BBC in Britain is known as the Beeb.

The Peeps fancies itself as a nation state, constantly at war with the government that votes the money to sustain it — rather like the constant conflict between Newfoundland and Ottawa. The money comes from Ottawa, the abuse from Newfoundland. It is a basic doctrine of the Peeps that while the Canadian union must be preserved, any government that happens to be elected must go. It is also taken for granted that, without the Peeps, the country would collapse into the arms of Uncle Sam and be subjected to the raping it would so richly deserve. To praise a government action, or even to be neutral about it, would be paid propaganda, hence not to be tolerated.

Talking about the Peeps is almost as futile as listening to it, though there is a good business to be made in fees for guest appearances, as generations of political reporters, pundits, university professors, and talking heads have discovered through the years. I myself have fed at that particular trough since the inception of television, never knowing who "they" were. "They" are the people who decide who goes on the network and who doesn't, without ever saying why, though it is helpful if you work for a Toronto paper, notably the *Globe and Mail*, which ensures that somebody in the Peeps will be aware of your existence.

But since I can't deal with the Peeps without sounding catty, and since everybody has his or her own opinion of it, let us turn to the *Globe and Mail*. And let us turn away just as quickly, if it's the national edition we're talking about, because it's thin pickings for a national institution, not to mention its claim to be one of the greatest newspapers in the world. The Metro edition of the *Globe* at least has some heft to it, despite having the nation's most anaemic comic section and a tendency to slash interesting dispatches while giving the dull stuff full play, especially in signed columns, sometimes labelled opinion and sometimes not. The *Globe*'s political cartoons contain as much mystery as its humour, particularly if you don't live in Toronto. The whole paper, full edition or the boiled-down version, is one big opinion piece — Toronto, the nation, and the world as perceived through the eyes of the *Globe and Mail*, and a largely humourless, disappointing scene it seems to be. The *Globe* has no funnybone, which is why we switched to the *Montreal Gazette* at our house, and have been laughing ever since.

At least the *Globe*, unlike the Peeps, doesn't keep shouting that, without it, the country would cease to exist. It just assumes that everybody knows that, and proceeds from there, displaying a pomposity so pervasive that thousands across the country believe it and don't regard the day as started until the

Globe is in their hands. I really believe it must be the Report on Business that does it, because it is several cuts above the rest of the paper and has no rivals, the business sections of most local newspapers being what they are. The joke there is that ever since the Report on Business became as thorough as it is, business in the country has been going to pot, and the national economy has seldom been in worse shape. The moral must be that the more we understand how business works, the worse we are at it.

The *Globe and Mail* operates without help from government, and hence has no reason to punish government the way the Peeps does to prove its independence. It puts the wood to government anyway, in line with the media doctrine that all elected representatives of the people are scoundrels, unless they happen to be in opposition to the government of the day. Next, please.

Maclean's also operates without a government subsidy, though it owes its existence as a newsmagazine to laws passed by Parliament, after intensive lobbying, to hobble Canadian editions of U.S. magazines. (Newspaper publishers in Canada achieved protection of their own from foreign ownership or competition, but they made a lot less fuss about it than *Maclean's* did, and it got a lot less media attention. Have you noticed that every power grab by media gets little play?) *Maclean's* costs $1.75, which boils down to ten cents a minute in terms of reading time, five minutes of that being for the Fotheringham column, unless he's being serious, when it's two.

The nation would almost certainly hang together without *Maclean's*, and people have been known to go for weeks and months without access to it, emerging with their Canadianism unimpaired. When people talk about *Maclean's* there is a tendency to talk about the good old days when the magazine had some meat in it, and was put out by legendary characters who all went on to fame somewhere else. Those were also the days when the magazine lost money, which tells us something, though nobody working there now seems to know just what. The ads in *Maclean's* are gorgeous, especially the ones for booze. But if you want to see really great ads, and grabby editorial content, try the sister publication *Chatelaine*. You get your money's worth there, even if you're a man, and nobody would think of saying the country would fold if *Chatelaine* did. And since it dwells so little on that old devil, identity, there is fun in its plentiful pages.

Which brings us to Air Canada, my home away from home, in whose seats I have logged most of my three million miles spent aloft. I began with the North Stars, our home-made transports that bridged continents and oceans, the only plane in which the passengers knew everything was okay as long as they could see the flames shooting out of the engines.

Air Canada long had the reputation as the only airline whose cabin crews gave passengers the feeling they were intruding — what the hell were all these people doing showing up on the airplane and cluttering up the aisles? The prevailing mood on the Air Canada jets is better, but it took a while — and during the learning years I invented the order of the broom, the symbol being a little witch's broom to be worn on the lapel, and offered to an offending flight attendant with the suggestion that he or she might want to fly outside awhile. By offending flight attendant, I mean one who is making the flight less pleasant than it otherwise would be, keeping in mind that I assume every flight is going to be my last, since I fail to understand what keeps aircraft aloft in the first place. I did not ask that they make flights better — I merely hoped they would not make them worse. Eventually, the atmosphere on board improved to the point where flight crews are so busy now, with masses of passengers, they don't have time to make themselves pleasant or objectionable, and most seem to have settled for neutrality, trying not to spill anything and telling us that every inconvenience is inflicted for our own comfort and safety, including those world's worst omelettes for breakfast.

No matter, they get us there, spurred by increasing competition from other airlines whose crews used to be more congenial but are now pretty much the same, through overwork. The country is easier to get around because of Air Canada, but the meals aren't any better and I'm still not sure it's a net gain to be able to visit three cities in a day, or for politicians to hit eight airports in eighteen hours during a campaign. You want to stay sane, go by train. You can also wind up dead on the rails, this being written in the wake of the great, awful, Hinton train wreck where people were snuffed eating breakfast in the dining car. You can get killed slipping in the bathtub, too.

In all my bellyaching about Air Canada, the only reform I ever succeeded in promoting was to get the airline to adopt pepper shakers that actually dispensed pepper. The original packages were paper tubes that became impregnated with oil from the pepper and wouldn't snap open, being soggy. I kept at this for years until finally they adopted a better model, and I asked why it had taken them so long. They said it was because they had a hangarful of the old ones and had to use them all up before making the change.

That was more than twenty years ago. Lo and behold, this very year they returned to the old tubular models of pepper shakers, thus denying me my one triumph in the skies. But I must say that the new version of the old shaker has kept its crispness, so it may be they have found a paper that is oil-proof, or they have taken all the oil out of the pepper.

There isn't too much to be said about Canadian National or Canadian Pacific as agencies of unity, though both companies say the country could not exist without them. CP says the country never would have been constructed without it, a claim no other agency makes apart from the Grit and Tory parties — but it is widely suspected that CP has been carried away by its own importance ever since Pierre Berton's book. Doubtless the Hudson's Bay Company will get the same notions when Peter Newman is finished with it, demonstrating yet again that the great romance of Canada is commerce, and that the most vivid line in our literature is the bottom line.

Now that the railways no longer carry people under their own label, passing the buck to VIA, they aren't as much fun as they used to be, to ride or to write about. I grew up in a Canadian Pacific town, Saint John, New Brunswick, hence hated the CN and all its works, including Moncton and Halifax. As a CPR passenger, I once helped snowball a CNR engineer out of his cab in Ottawa's Union Station. It is a feeling that has endured to this day — Canadian Pacific seems to be lean and right, and CN fat and wrong. The same thing happened in our family with respect to cars — father once sold Fords and always drove them when I was part of the household, and we learned to boo Chevs and Plymouths. I drive Ford products to this day, convinced they have the right stuff, even against foreign competition. I loved my Mazda Rotary in its time, two rusted-out bodies ago.

When the railways carried passengers, everybody knew who the presidents of the lines were, and there were always big fusses in Parliament, where the biggest committee rooms were known as the Railway Rooms. They're not called that any more because there's no romance in freight, and nobody thinks of having committee rooms named for the buses or the planes.

CN and CP tell us they hold the country together by moving goods, when their trains aren't off the rails, and they make much about their telecommunications and diverse operations such as trucking and hotels. But they don't build hotels the way they used to, much less terminals, be they for buses or aircraft. Windsor Station in Montreal was and is in a class by itself, even if few trains go there any more, and the Château Frontenac is a source of national pride, the greatest of those fantasy confections built by those old pirates who put the railways through. Compared to the European and Japanese railways, though, these guys are just dabblers, and the foreign lines have kept their place as movers of people, in great comfort at high speed, and as much safety as is possible when the scenery is a blur.

The Trans-Canada Highway probably has done more for the country than all of the above, in terms of what the average person knows. If you haven't driven the length of it you must have used some sections, unless you're a northerner or live in the Magdalen Islands. Of course, too much of the Trans-Canada Highway is in Ontario, which can't be helped, and there's only one of it, which we could do something about if we wanted to — such as build another highway, to today's standards rather than those of the 1950s. Failing which, what about a bicycle path along the present route?

The road is a killer, but it's a darling drive most of the way, and most places it's the best road around, or was when it was built, proving that when a federal government puts its mind to something, it can make good things happen. Not as good as the U.S. Interstates, those expensive wonders of the motoring world, but good, just the same, even if New Brunswickers used the early pavement to dry dulse on.

Having said which, I have to confess that my own favourite drives, here at home or anywhere in the world I've been, have nothing to do with the Trans-Canada Highway. They are, in order of their beauty and the fun of driving them, the highway from Lake Louise to Jasper (both ways), the drive from Vancouver to Squamish and Whistler, the Cabot Trail, the Gaspé Trail, the Saint John River road in New Brunswick, and the whole stretch of the Eastern Shore and the South Shore of Nova Scotia. I'll listen to arguments about the Rhine and the Loire valleys, the Cotswolds, the sheep trails of the Highlands, the Kerry Ring, and the Khyber Pass. Having driven them all, I won't yield our best to any of them. The Grand Canyon is nice but you can't drive through it, or even to it any more. I applaud the redwood forests of Oregon and the niceness of New England, and I could sit a long time in Nantucket. But we're talking about pleasurable drives here, and we've got them, with even some good inns and watering places along the way. Still, it's a long, weary way from Thunder Bay to Winnipeg.

That leaves the Canadian Press, another agency that fancies itself as the glue that holds us together, the assertion of our identity, the great viewer of the world through Canadian eyes, though most of its international stuff is bought from the Americans, the British, and the French. It was ever thus, and we wouldn't have a national news agency at all if the governments hadn't subsidized it in the 1920s to get the wordage across the great open spaces. There was even a subsidy from the British government well into the 1930s. CP has always had trouble with the two solitudes here at home, doing such a poor job on covering postwar Quebec that the Quiet Revolution took the rest of the country by surprise, very nearly doing us in.

Whether the nation is better off or worse off for the Canadian Press having existed is open to debate, though hardly anybody bothers to discuss it. The writing is more sprightly than it used to be, matching the topspin put on stories by the special writers for Southam, the *Toronto Star*, and the Sun papers, and a mention in the CP file still can bring more nationwide exposure than is available in any other way apart from the flickering, fleeting images on the TV networks. But it seldom gets into the Toronto papers, which at times have dabbled with the idea of dropping CP altogether. The Toronto *Sun* actually tried it, but lost a bundle, and came home to the cheap and reliable, both terms being relative.

Yes, the country could do without CP — the publishers who own it have often thought of folding it and were on the verge of doing so in 1950 when workers were rumbling about a union. I saw the shadow plan, and it was simple — dissolve CP and set up another news exchange just like it.

So what holds us together? The Bay? Bell? Canadian Tire? Big Macs? Labatts? Molsons? Gretzky? The CN Tower, Expo 86, the Calgary Winter Olympics? Love/hate of the Yanks? None of the above? Great!

Funny country, eh?

Index

Air Canada, 129, 205, 208–9
Aldred, Joel, 86
Allen, Ralph, 181, 183, 184, 186–94, 199
An, Mr., 26
Anderson, Ronald, 199
Anderson, Torchy, 5
Andrew, Prince, 43, 146
Atkins, Norman, 121
Atwood, Margaret, 38
Auger, Fred, 110
Axworthy, Tom, 121

Balfour, St. Clair, 4
Bankok syndrome, 76
Banks, Hal, 52
Barrett, Silby, 135–37
Barrette, Antonio, 106–7
Bassett, John, 165
Beaton, Al, 108
Bennett, R. B., 67, 144
Bennett, W. A. C., 155
Berton, Pierre, 205, 209
Bienstalk, Nathan, 182
Black, George, 37
Blackburn, Clyde, 13
Blackmore, John, 41
Blakeley, Allan, 93
Borden, Sir Robert, 134
Bourne, Robin, 97
Bracken, John, 124–26
Broadbent, Ed, 16, 167
Buckley, Christopher, 186
Burger, Madame, 27
Burns, General E. L. M., 2

CBC, 1, 9, 29, 59, 173–75, 182, 200–6
Calgary Herald, 190

Calgary Stampede, 38
Callwood, June, 133
Camp, Dalton, 121, 165
Canadian Clubs, 201–2
Canadian National Railways, 205, 209–10
Canadian Pacific Railway, 205, 209–10
Canadian Press, 1, 5, 184, 211–12
Caouette, Réal, 39, 100–1
Carney, Pat, 2
Case, Garfield, 126
Champlain, Samuel de, 57
Charles, Prince, 6, 16, 100, 146
Chatelaine, 54, 207–8
Chevaldayoff, Wayne, 199
Chivas Regal, 53
Chrétien, Jean, 7, 9, 45, 129
Chronicle-Herald, Halifax, 4
Churchill, Winston, 202
Clark, Hugh, 144
Clark, Joe, 4, 15, 16, 18, 21, 41, 51, 52, 55, 56, 72, 95, 97, 101, 140
Coates, Robert, 30
Cogger, Michel, 20
Colbert, Claudette, 52
Coldwell, M. J., 200
Coles Bookstores, 7
Connolley, John, 126
Copps, Sheila, 16
Coutts, Jim, 98, 121
Creery, Tim, 31
Crerar, General H. D. G., 125
Cronkite, Walter, 182
Crosbie, John, 29, 51
Crouse, Lloyd, 41–43
Currie, Sir Arthur, 135

Danson, Barney, 90

213

215